Technology
&Spirituality

Technology
&Spirituality

How the
Information
Revolution
Affects Our
Spiritual Lives

Stephen K. Spyker

Walking Together, Finding the Way®
SKYLIGHT PATHS®
PUBLISHING
Woodstock, Vermont

Technology & Spirituality:
How the Information Revolution Affects Our Spiritual Lives

2007 First Printing
© 2007 by Stephen K. Spyker

Library of Congress Cataloging-in-Publication Data

Spyker, Stephen K.
Technology & spirituality : how the information revolution affects our spiritual lives / Stephen K. Spyker.
    p. cm.
Includes bibliographical references.
ISBN-13: 978-1-59473-218-8 (hardcover)
ISBN-10: 1-59473-218-3 (hardcover)
1.   Technology—Religious aspects—Christianity. I. Title. II. Title:
Technology and spirituality.
BR115.T42S69 2007
261.5'6—dc22

                         2007001583

10 9 8 7 6 5 4 3 2 1

Manufactured in the United States of America
❀ Printed on recycled paper
Jacket Design: Tim Holtz

SkyLight Paths Publishing is creating a place where people of different spiritual traditions come together for challenge and inspiration, a place where we can help each other understand the mystery that lies at the heart of our existence.

SkyLight Paths sees both believers and seekers as a community that increasingly transcends traditional boundaries of religion and denomination—people wanting to learn from each other, *walking together, finding the way.*

SkyLight Paths, "Walking Together, Finding the Way" and colophon are trademarks of LongHill Partners, Inc., registered in the U.S. Patent and Trademark Office.

Walking Together, Finding the Way®
Published by SkyLight Paths Publishing
A Division of LongHill Partners, Inc.
Sunset Farm Offices, Route 4, P.O. Box 237
Woodstock, VT 05091
Tel: (802) 457-4000   Fax: (802) 457-4004
www.skylightpaths.com

CONTENTS

Acknowledgments   vii

0   Introduction: Redefining the Boundaries   1

1   'Tis a Gift to Be Simple   17

2   Finding Our Way   35

3   Virtual Village   51

4   I Am My iPod   67

5   Arigato, Roboto   83

6   I Can't Drive 55   101

7   Neutrons, Networks, and New Models of God   115

8   The Truth Shall Set You Free   133

Notes   148

Suggestions for Further Reading   157

ACKNOWLEDGMENTS

Kids whose worst subject in school was English don't grow up to write books without a lot of help. The list of people I ought to thank (or blame) for getting me here is probably endless, but I'll name just a few of the more notorious.

Tom Mullen for demonstrating how writing can be a ministry, John Miller for allowing me to believe I could write, James McElhinney for teaching me to tell the truth, no matter what, Haven Kimmel and Joe Armstrong for showing me how, Jay Marshall for the opportunity, Steve Reid for the encouragement, Stephanie Ford for the path, and all my friends, enemies, students, teachers, mentors, and colleagues at Earlham School of Religion, Bethany Theological Seminary, and Ball State University for giving me a life.

I owe a special debt of gratitude to my editor, Mark Ogilbee, whose vision has guided this work from conception to completion (and persistently saved me from myself), and to my wife, Donna, whose undying love and support has, quite literally, made this project possible.

0

INTRODUCTION

Redefining the Boundaries

Most of us are not terribly reflective about the technologies we use. We may be hesitant in our approach or slow to adapt, but sooner or later we blindly accept whatever technology comes along, acting as if we believe, however skeptical we might have been at first, that it will make our lives easier, better, more interesting or rewarding, that we will be better or happier or more valued human beings because of some newfangled way of doing something.

At the same time we tend to dismiss the power of technology too lightly, acting as though it doesn't really affect us. We know it affects our lives, to be sure, but it doesn't really affect *us*, does it? Deep down, our identity and our relation to God and to other human beings is unaffected by the whirlwind of technological change that surrounds us, right?

If you truly want to believe that, read no further. Set this book down, walk away quietly, and I'll cause you no further discomfort. Then again, you might want to read on a bit, but only if you're willing to face the uncomfortable reality that we

1

are what we eat, that the technologies we "consume" (and in the lexicon of the technocrats we are all merely "consumers" or "users"; think about the implications of that for a minute) in some important sense determine who we are.

My goal in writing this book is to help us[1] gain a deeper understanding of how emerging technologies affect our spirituality, how we can learn to live with (or without) them better, and how we can develop a relationship with technology that will help nurture our spiritual being. If I am successful, this book will empower us to make some good choices regarding our personal use of technology and our attitude toward it.

OIL AND WATER

One could argue that spirituality and technology are like oil and water; that both might be interesting and important areas of inquiry on their own, but that one has little to do with the other. I categorically reject this notion, and I hope that over the course of your reading you will come to reject it also. But first let's take a look at what we really mean by technology.

Technology is a word whose Greek roots are quite familiar. The *-ology* part comes from the Greek word *logos*, an important concept in ancient philosophy and modern Christian spirituality. It is normally translated as "word" but the meaning runs deeper, such as in the Gospel of John where the *w* is capitalized. We get some flavor of this deeper meaning in modern expressions such as "give me the word on the street." In common use it simply means "the study of," as in the words *biology, psychology, sociology, astrology, numerology,* and so on ad infinitum; you can make up your own words using *–ology,* and most people will instinctively know precisely what you mean.

The Greek *technikos*—in addition to the various forms and permutations of *technology,* such as *technical, technician, technobabble* (the stuff they say on *Star Trek*), *technophobia*—

also shows up in the word *technique,* which perhaps better points to its true meaning, most closely approximated by the English words *art* and *skill.* This understanding helps to correct one of the common misconceptions about technology, namely that it deals strictly with the material. Naturally, we associate technology with contraptions, gizmos, or gadgets. We think of science fiction scenarios: monstrous machines, robots, mountains of wire, and sprawling wastelands of complicated equipment. In the minds of many, technology is cold and capricious, all head, no heart, and no soul. One might even say that technology is the antithesis of humanity.

Nothing could be further from the truth. Technology is the study of human art and skill. In the struggle to differentiate human beings from other animals, anthropologist have sometimes pointed to our propensity to fashion and use tools. Think of paintbrushes and pens, not just screwdrivers and hammers.

But technology is not our tools; it is how we *create* and *use* tools. In a nutshell, technology is part of what defines us; it is part of what makes us human. More than that, the technologies we adopt affect the very type of humans we become. The tools we choose to use and how we use them affect how we think, how we make decisions, how we relate to one another, how we construct knowledge, even how we think about God. This connection between technology and anthropology is not always obvious. We tend to think of our human identity as some sort of absolute. After all, we created our technology, it didn't create us, right?

True enough, but when we study the history of human thought, with a mind to concurrent technological development, it's not hard to see that over a sufficiently long period of time any major development in technology will eventually affect our sense of identity and our engagement with the world. Even outside the historical record it's easy to imagine how technology might change our outlook. Humans with the ability to make and control fire would have a fundamentally different outlook on the world—and attitude toward their role in it—than humans without such technology. From there it's equally easy to speculate how the wheel, agriculture, architecture, printing, chemical engineering, or just about any other major break-through in technology would have a similar sort of revolution-ary impact on our sense of self and our experience of the world.

We're right in the thick of such a revolution today. A num-ber of technological breakthroughs in the last half century, prob-ably starting with the invention of the digital computer and the transistor in the 1940s and 1950s—which came together in the 1970s in the microprocessor—have been radically transforming communications technology and essentially reinventing infor-mation technology. I tend to call these various breakthroughs "emerging" technologies, though some are much more devel-oped than others. They mostly revolve around computers and the Internet in one way or another, but it would be a mistake to identify either as the main technology driving the revolution.

It's not just the personal computer or just the Internet that is transforming our world; it's the whole gestalt. Indeed, part of the task before us is to conceptualize how all these emerging technologies differentiate and fit together, and where they are all taking us. This movement has been referred to variously in the literature, but one concept that seems to have caught on, and which brings the proper perspective, is that we are transi-tioning from the industrial age (which followed the Iron Age, Bronze Age, and Stone Age) to the "information age." In an effort to invoke this sense of fundamental paradigmatic shift in our culture, I have come to refer to the onslaught of these var-ious technologies collectively as the *information revolution.*

That's enough for now on technology, but what of spiritu-ality? What do we mean, what are we talking about, when we speak of "spirituality"? If my central thesis is that technology and spirituality have a relationship, that they are not like oil and water but rather that they affect one another, that they do "mix" in ways that are worthy of consideration and study, then I need to make some attempt to define spirituality, if not for all purposes, then at least for the purposes of this book.

Etymology is of limited help here. The word *spirit* is generally associated with the animating force of life, the uniquely dualistic understanding that we are material beings trapped in the material world, bags of water and other chemicals inhabited by a superior "spirit," a "ghost in the machine," if you will. That's fine, if that's your philosophical take on the human condition, but it's not mine and it doesn't have to be yours in order to have some understanding of spirituality.

I believe that we *are* souls, not bodies *with* a soul. I believe that we are *spiritual beings*, not spiritually possessed material beings. With this understanding, it's clear that everything that affects you, affects you spiritually; there is no reality independent from spiritual reality. Madonna got it exactly wrong: we are not material girls living in a material world, we are spiritual beings living in a spiritual world, a world where those ultimate truths we tend to categorize under the heading of "religion" have real and important consequences for us and for everyone else.

A colleague of mine, someone who teaches Christian spirituality for a living, defines spirituality as "how matters of ultimate concern find expression in your life." That's the best general definition for spirituality I've ever encountered, and the one I'd like you to keep in mind as you read. In other words, I'd like you to think about what your ultimate concerns are, what truths you hold most dear, or what, in the final analysis, is most important to you. You might find these matters of ultimate concern concisely defined for you in a religious tradition, or you might still be searching; you might be comfortable speaking of these matters as your "faith tradition," or you might have strong objections to that sort of language; you might have a rich dogmatic or creedal understanding of the truth, or you might have a long list of rich questions or paradoxical conclusions whose mysteries you struggle to live into. Personally, I would want you to have both, but whatever you have, however you define your faith or doubts, they find some sort of expression in your life. If you have found truth, how do you express these truths to yourself and to others? If you have questions, how do you ask these questions and where do you look for answers? This is your spirituality.

I will refer to my own religious beliefs or tradition (Quaker/Christian) when I think it might help clarify what I'm trying to say, or as an example of how a general principle might apply in a specific context, or when I simply can't help myself, but I can't presume that your religious convictions parallel mine. Spirituality—though it is a nice word that helps us to transcend some of the differences between various religious understandings—needs to be defined within a religious understanding or faith tradition. Hence, I will often speak of spirituality as if we all know what that word means and as if we were all talking about the same thing, but don't be fooled. Each of us will have to define spirituality for ourselves; each of us needs to do a little interpretive, hermeneutic exercise every time we see that word in the text and decide what, both within the context of the text and within our religious convictions, it means for us.

WHY THIS BOOK?

I have lived my life at the nexus of spirituality and technology. I'm an engineer and technologist by disposition, forever tinkering, troubleshooting, inventing, designing, and critiquing the status quo. Some of my earliest childhood memories are of dismantling and (sometimes successfully) reassembling, rebuilding, modifying, or otherwise "fixing" clocks, bicycles, lawn mowers, flashlights, radios, televisions—essentially anything I could get my hands on, often in secret. As a musically challenged guitarist and saxophonist, I quite naturally fell into the role of equipment manager/roadie for several small-time local rock bands. I fell in love with television broadcasting in college, partly because being around all those lights, cables, and black boxes felt as natural as rock and roll. I majored in broadcasting, picked up an FCC (Federal Communications Commission) license to operate the college's television transmitter, and had a long, comfortable, and interesting career as a broadcast/video engineer.

Likewise, religion has always fascinated me. While I was still in my first decade of life I tried to read the Bible straight through, tried my best to be a devout Methodist, and even thought God was calling me to the ministry. As I entered adolescence I grew disenchanted with the organized church, decided I was an atheist, then an agnostic (or was it the other way around?), and, eventually, a Buddhist. Over time I essentially abandoned religion in any practiced or disciplined way, but I remained curious. And if I was dubious of those who claimed to have answers, I still considered theological questions the most important and profound of any that could be asked. Eventually I found my way back to Christianity and discovered, to my surprise, that I was a Quaker.

I always figured the engineering thing was temporary; I wanted to do something that *mattered*, something that had *meaning*. I started to feel a renewed calling to ministry in my thirties and a way opened for me to enter seminary. I figured I was probably the first engineer to ever go to seminary, but I gradually discovered there are a lot of us geeks out there who love technology and love God. Go figure.

Like any good education, seminary just left me asking better questions and hungrier than ever for learning. When I began studying computer technology again, more or less on a whim, it was like coming home. It felt like rock and roll. As much as I loved seminary, as much as I loved God, *this* was my element. During the vocational discernment process at seminary, people often talked of "pursuing your bliss," and this appeared to be it.

Technology jazzed me, it rocked, it was what I was born to do, and I missed it.

So I entered a doctoral program in education and information/communication science, hoping I might someday land a job at a seminary somewhere helping folks with educational technology. I no sooner imagined the job than I had it, and I started full-time work the very same week I started coursework.

For the next three years I spent my days at one institution of higher education and my evenings at another, one unabashedly religious, the other decidedly secular. I felt like I was commuting between two completely different worlds. In one world, matters of the spirit were supreme. There was communal worship at least once and more typically twice a day, classes and business meetings usually began with a period of silent worship and/or prayer, and we spoke casually (dare I say irreverently) of the Divine. Science, mathematics, and, especially, technology were viewed with suspicion at best.

In the other world, opening a class, let alone a business meeting, with prayer would be unthinkable, not to mention grounds for a lawsuit. But the differences went deeper than just the familiar compartmentalization of spirituality. It was more a matter of how knowledge was defined and valued. Matters of the spirit were cause for suspicion, bemusement, and, ultimately, dismissal. Mathematics and science, far from being perceived as crude, cold, and dangerous, were embraced as the final and only real arbitrators of truth, and technology was our god.[2] By putting all the information ever created everywhere a mouse click away, it promised to make us all better and wiser, more competent and more powerful. By giving us instantaneous access to each other, it promised to improve our relations and mutual understanding. By improving our productivity through more efficient information management, it promised to increase our aggregate wealth. As technologists, we were the high priests and keepers of the sacred knowledge.

It made for an interesting commute. On good days it felt like I had found a graceful balance between my spiritual and philotechnical natures. On bad days it felt like I was being torn apart; whatever I did of value in one world was derided in the other. I was split in two, and, like all pilgrims, I yearned for wholeness.

If life has taught me anything it's that I'm not unique; I can't be the only one who feels this split, this divide between a love of God and a love of technology. And so this book is at some level an attempt to help me and those like me find wholeness, a way of bringing together our two worlds. That said, I hope also to reach folks who perhaps don't share my love of technology. In truth, I'm a little ambivalent of it myself, and if I've been a reluctant champion of technology in spiritual circles, I've been a bit of a downer among technophiles, quick with a caveat or a cautionary tale. It is said that the prophetic task is to comfort the afflicted and afflict the comfortable. I'm no prophet, but in some small way I hope to calm the fears of the technophobic, yet curb the enthusiasm of the technological utopians.

TAKING THE RED PILL

This isn't my first book on spirituality and technology; my dissertation was entitled *Spirituality and Technology: A Study in Frontiers* (Ball State University, 2004), and the structure of this book is loosely based on an analytical matrix introduced in the concluding chapter of that one; hence, some explanation of "the matrix"[3] I suggested in that earlier work should prove helpful here.

Matrix is a word with a lot of shades of meaning depending upon your field. Not surprisingly, the sense of the word I had in mind when I started using it comes more from mathematics and computer science, specifically the idea of a set of the intersections formed by nonparallel lines. The metaphor I had in mind was of looking at phenomena from as many different "angles" as possible in order to build a more accurate picture.

But a matrix is also the substance out of which something else originates. In this sense, matrix is a synonym for *womb*. Technology originates, or exists in any event, not in a vacuum but in a matrix of complex and interrelated human and scientific phenomena. It's my observation that we often choose to ignore the myriad of complex and often subtle factors that describe or define a given technology, and that by so doing we often miss the real impact these technologies have on our lives, particularly our spiritual lives. We put simple, one-dimensional labels, like "high tech," on things. These labels aren't very helpful in analyzing or describing a particular technology—calling something "high tech" tells us little other than we don't understand it and probably don't want to. Worse, it leads us to ask naive questions, such as, "Do high-tech devices interfere with your spiritual life?" or "Has our world become too high tech?" or even "Should my church go high tech?" These questions are simply too vague to spawn very meaningful discussions, let alone return useful, practical answers.

The matrix is intended to do the opposite: it is a tool to get us to ask good questions and spawn meaningful discussions. With any luck it will also help find good, practical answers—like whether or not to buy an LCD projector for your church, whether your prayer group would benefit from a Web presence, or whether you should give up your cell phone for Lent—but this is not primarily a book designed to provide answers. It is a book that, if at all successful, will get you to ask some deep questions that may not otherwise have occurred to you. And as long as I'm talking about what this book isn't, this is decidedly *not* a "how to" book. Along the way, I hope you learn a thing or two about the information revolution, but this is not "Everything spiritual people ought to know about technology but are afraid to ask" or "How anybody can do anything they want with technology."

Even so, the matrix is entirely utilitarian; it is an analytical approach, a conceptual framework for examining important principles. It also helps me provide some structure for framing what would otherwise be an impossibly open-ended discussion. I ask you to accept it only to the extent that it is useful in helping you think about the issues under discussion.

The matrix consists of eight "lenses"—though you could as easily think of them as windows or angles of view—through which we can "look" at any given technology or application thereof. Each lens of the matrix gives us a way of evaluating technologies and their applications with a particular set of properties or effects in mind.

FINDING FRONTIERS

I spoke before of technology and spirituality as oil and water and suggested that it was an inappropriate metaphor; that, unlike oil and water, technology and spirituality can and do mix. As an alternative, think of spirituality and technology as two countries. Normally these countries keep comfortably to themselves. Both are vast, and no one person living in them will ever see or truly know them in their entirety. In spite of this vastness, the frontiers of each appear to be fairly well established; we can cross the frontier from one country to another, but when we do we're quite aware of the crossing. Afterward, there's little or no ambiguity as to which country we are in.

But let's linger at the frontier for a minute. We might find places where the boundary is not as clear as we thought or where it appears completely arbitrary or even misplaced. We might find fences that need to be moved, gated, or torn down, places where there is, or could be, interaction between the spiritual and the technical. By picking up this book you have climbed up onto one of the fences that divides technology from spirituality. By reading this far you've sojourned along the frontier, and by now I hope you're thinking about maybe knocking some holes in that fence. That's the point of the *boundary* lens, to get us to gaze upon the frontier, to become aware of the fences that unwittingly influence our path, and to consider how that path might vary if we simply ignored the boundary.[4]

As we continue our journey, examining various emerging technologies and their spiritual ramifications, we will discover other frontiers, other places where we have put our thoughts and ideas into boxes in order to make more sense out of the world or in order that we might have meaningful conversations. It is not that these boxes are bad, or that "thinking outside the box"[5] is always a good thing. The point is to identify the frontiers, take a good honest look at the fences, and know that we can hop them or even tear them down in places. Put another way: it's not that boundaries are bad; what's bad is walking what we think is the only available path because we lack the imagination to envision crossing over.

The frontier between spirituality and technology is not fixed, and whatever fences lie between them are constructed largely in our minds, full of holes, easily breached, and, in some places, in need of being torn down. Such is the task before us.

EMPLOYING THE MATRIX

Each chapter of this book is an examination of the relationship between technology and spirituality through a particular lens of the matrix. This structure will allow us to explore some of the more interesting developments in the information revolution and speculate on how they might be affecting us and our spirituality and will also demonstrate, by way of example, how the matrix works, and how you might use it in your own analysis.

The first of the eight lenses is called *boundary*. It has been introduced here, in the introduction, but boundary is a theme that carries throughout the book. The idea of the boundary lens is that we examine and question the definitions, the categories, the fences we put around our thoughts in order to make sense of the world and keep us from going insane. Using the boundary lens means that we question the boundaries, the frontiers, and ask what would happen if we rearranged them a bit, redefined them, or even ignored them.

The boundary lens is the place where we begin, at zero, the long overlooked number where counting truly begins. Without the boundary lens, humans would never have conceived of the number zero, and our mathematics would be forever stilted. It took someone willing to color outside the lines, someone willing to ask silly questions, someone a little "crazy" to ever think we needed zero. Zero is just nothing, isn't it? We use numbers to count things, so why would we want a number that stands for nothing? In this respect, "using the boundary lens" is just another way of talking about critical thinking, the type of thinking that questions common-sense interpretations of things, such as the notion that we start counting with one and that nothing is not anything and therefore we don't need a number for it. And that is why, in case you were wondering, I call this introduction "chapter 0."

In chapter 1, "'Tis a Gift to Be Simple," we'll examine the concept of *simplicity* within religious thought and how it relates to our use of technology. We'll take a look at traditional communal responses to technology, including those of the Amish, the Shakers, and the much maligned (and misunderstood) Luddites. Simplicity is a big part of what engineers call "elegance." It is a critical factor in all good design, and it, or more precisely the lack of it, is a big factor in our current difficulties in relating to emerging technologies.

Chapter 2, "Finding Our Way," continues on an historical theme, demonstrating how technologies in the past have transformed our world, and consequently changed our thinking and our spirituality. Even though these revolutionary technologies have been lauded and conspicuously celebrated, their effects on our culture are sometimes less obvious, hence the

connection with the concept of *transparency*, the third lens of
the matrix.[6] But the real connection to transparency, and to the
technology alluded to in the chapter's title, comes when we
examine emerging search and data–processing technologies.
These technologies are practically invisible to most of us, working behind the scenes in ways that do not require our thought
or attention, but they promise to bring about a revolution
at least as sweeping as the historical examples cited in the
chapter.[7]

In chapter 3, "Virtual Village," we'll examine how the
information revolution is changing our perception of *community*, particularly in cyberspace. "Community" is a term that
gets tossed around a lot, and unquestionably there are communities of various sorts in cyberspace, but can we find true spiritual community online? Yes, I will argue. But what about
geography? Has the Internet rendered it obsolete? If the mountain won't come to Mohammad, should he just visit its website?
These are the sorts of questions we are led to explore by examining technology through the lens of community. The underlying question posed in this chapter is where reality lies along
the continuum between the material and the virtual.

Chapter 4, "I Am My iPod," takes up the theme of *identity*. As a technical support person, I've had a lot of opportunity
to witness how people "get along" with their technology and
how the technologies we adopt get wrapped up in how we see
ourselves. In this chapter we will examine how technology is
evolving and how we might be evolving in response to it.

Chapter 5, "Arigato, Roboto," continues with the theme
(lens) of identity, but shifts the focus more to the nature of our
relationship with our machines. How can we better get along with
our gadgets? Can we have a fulfilling *personal* relationship with a
technological device? Does your computer have a soul? Will it
someday? No discussion of spirituality and technology could pretend to be complete without taking a hard look at artificial intel-

ligence (AI), considering its implications, and speculating on how it might affect our roles as both creators and creatures.

In Chapter 6, "I Can't Drive 55,"[8] we evaluate how technology, particularly in the way it is marketed, plays off our desire for speed, both literally and metaphorically. Technological advances often revolve around a promise to get us where we want to go more quickly or, often, instantaneously. But just as often, they succeed only in making life more hectic, leaving us with a deeper desire to slow down. The role technology plays in addressing our conflicting heartfelt desires involving space (as in "miles") and time (as in "per hour") comes to the forefront when we look through the lens of *velocity*.

Chapter 7, "Neutrons, Networks, and New Models of God," is all about connections and *connectivity*. A quick walk down any city street or a brief visit to a typical work environment will tell you we are living in a hyperconnected age. But what are all these connections doing to us spiritually? Are they binding us together in a nurturing community, or are we just so terrified of being alone in our own skin that we need to make a phone call or send an e-mail every few minutes in order to avoid any time whatsoever in the desert, where we might have to confront our daemons or rely utterly on God?

The other phenomenon that pops into focus through the connectivity lens, and is briefly introduced in chapter 7, is the emerging science of networks. One can amass impressive statistics about how much data is available on the Internet and how many people depend on it or make their living from it, but the truly revolutionary aspect of the Internet is the network of connections and how they, and other networks, behave as an entity. We are just beginning to understand some of the implications of this phenomenon.

In chapter 8, "The Truth Shall Set You Free," we'll examine what may be the ultimate promise of all technologies: *liberty*. Does technology really set us free, or, on the contrary, are we just addicted to it? Both, I will claim. "Labor-saving" has been the adjective applied to most of the fruit of the industrial and technological revolutions, but as photographer and inventor Eadweard Muybridge pointed out more than a hundred years ago, these gizmos and gadgets are never truly labor-saving; for the most part, people work just as hard now as they ever did. What these widgets and black boxes really are is consumption-enabling devices; we still work hard, but we have a lot more stuff to show for it.[9] But does all this stuff liberate us, or do we just become the prisoners of our possessions?

When we evaluate technological applications or our personal use of a given technology, we should hold them to the promises its proponents make and evaluate them the way I once heard a U.S. senator say we should evaluate U.S. Supreme Court candidates: ask yourself, "At the end of the day, am I more free or less free because of this gadget or activity or practice?" If the answer is "less free," perhaps you're better off without it. Easy for me to say. Addiction is a powerful thing.

To be clear, the matrix is intended for evaluation, not diagnosis. It's something you might consider using from time to time as you try to make decisions regarding a particular technology and its role in your life, not something like the Meyers-Briggs personality inventory test that's designed to provide insight on your own attitudes, though you might discover some of those along the way. At the end of chapter 8, we'll take one last look at the matrix and get more specific on how you might use it to evaluate your own relationship with technology on an ongoing basis. Until then, I'll mostly avoid referring to the matrix or to lenses as such; I don't want to exaggerate their importance or allow them to get in the way of the material and the issues we need to consider if we're going to understand how technology is affecting our spiritual lives.

So are you ready for a little fence cutting?

1

'TIS A GIFT TO BE SIMPLE

'Tis the gift to be loved and that love to return,
'Tis the gift to be taught and a richer gift to learn,
And when we expect of others what we try to live each day,
Then we'll all live together and we'll all learn to say:
"When true simplicity is gained,
To bow and to bend we shan't be ashamed."

—Joseph Brackett Jr., 1848[1]

Are you a Luddite, fearful of technology, or maybe a little hostile toward it? I meet people who claim to be all the time. Folks seem particularly willing to admit being Luddites once they know what I do for a living. I say "admit" because they tend to use the term as a pejorative, while at the same time taking a sort of strange pride in their ignorance of things technical, the way one might brag about his or her inability to dance or recall names. What they seem to be saying is, in effect, "I don't know diddly about computer stuff, but I'm okay with that, since it's all a bunch of hooey anyway." I'm okay with it too, I guess. I'm a bit of a Luddite myself.

Or perhaps you're a techtopian, one who gets all fired up on technology, confident that it has the potential to solve many of the world's most plaguing problems and create a better life for everyone. I'm definitely a techtopian; I see a lot of good things happening with technology in the world today, and I see a lot more potential good unrealized.

So how can I claim to be both a Luddite and a techtopian? Which view is more realistic? Is technology something that will solve all the world's problems, bringing about a brighter tomorrow, or is it just leading us straight down the information highway to hell?

Well, neither, of course. If we approach the question of technology and spirituality with this sort of bipolar Luddite-techtopian dialectic we'll end up nowhere. I won't even suggest that there's a continuum between the two. Technology is not the solution to all our problems any more than it's the cause of them. Being "pro-technology," or "anti-technology," or even claiming to be neutral is meaningless. The real picture is much more complicated than a simple, one-dimensional continuum between pro- and anti-technology, and we can begin to get a better idea of that picture by taking a semi-historical look at three groups of people. Each group is perceived to be radically anti-technology, but upon closer examination, each can give us unique insight on how people of faith might come to terms with the onslaught of new technologies and come to have a relationship with technology that nurtures their spirituality.

GOOD KING LUDD

Etymologically, *Luddites* is a moniker that, depending upon whom you believe, was either taken by or applied to a perceived "organization" of nineteenth-century saboteurs. My guess is that the Luddites were not terribly organized, though there were undoubtedly isolated conspiracies here and there. What is clear is that large, sometimes riotous groups of English subjects took to smashing knitting machines and other industrial equipment, and that they did so in protest of the deplorable working conditions brought on by the Industrial Revolution. They were imagined to be led, or at least inspired, by the notorious Ned Ludd, a.k.a. King Ludd or Captain Ludd, a gremlinish rascal who was typically accused of being responsible when knitting machines were demolished under otherwise mysterious circumstances.[2]

What had the Luddites so hot under the collar was not that they disliked technology, per se, but that textile machines were taking away their livelihood. The Luddites made the entirely reasonable observation that technology was supposed to serve human needs, not vice versa, and on that central philosophical point I stand with them in unequivocal solidarity. So would most people, we can hope.

I'll leave it to others to decide whether the rather violent means of the Luddites were justified, or at all effective for that matter, but, for better or worse, modern-day Luddites don't usually smash things. In fact, I suspect twenty-first-century Luddites bear little resemblance to their historical counterparts. It was economics, not technology, that had the original Luddites all excited. I don't think they would have gotten upset if someone had given their kids a Game Boy or if they suddenly were confronted with a microwave oven; it was their jobs and their stomachs they were worried about, not technology in any abstract sense.

Conversely, claiming to be a Luddite today is unmistakably anti-technology. When our contemporaries claim Ludditehood, they may mean any number of interesting things, but there's no doubt that they are expressing some sort of negative feeling toward technology. It's not always clear which technologies they have in mind (I don't think I've ever met a self-proclaimed Luddite who refused to ride in a car or use a telephone, for example), but they leave little doubt that they are somehow opposed to or bothered by technology.

The fact that the Luddites came and went nearly two hundred years ago shades the modern meaning as well. There's a certain backwardness implied by "Luddite," hearkening back to an earlier era before all "this stuff" came along. Sometimes people cop to Ludditeness in an apologetic tone, as if to say, "I just can't keep up with all this stuff, I guess I'm just too old-fashioned or simple-minded to deal with it." They don't like something because they are a little frightened by it. They are frightened by it because it's new, and therefore they're ignorant of it. They feel a little guilty because somewhere in the back of their minds they think they ought to know more about it, but that just feeds the fear, which encourages the dislike, which reinforces the ignorance, and so it goes.

Behind this modern usage of the name is the romantic perception that the Luddites were backward yokels fighting a hopeless battle against the relentless forces of the Industrial Revolution, but in truth the Luddites were neither anti-progress nor anti-technology. The machines they took to smashing produced textile products that were unquestionably inferior to the handmade goods they replaced. Though industrialization would lead to cheaper consumer goods, and arguably leave the working class all "better off" in the long run, that was hardly obvious at the time. Perhaps it still isn't. To the Luddites, and to many of us today, the Industrial Revolution hardly seemed like progress. From the Luddite perspective, industrialization served mainly to further enrich wealthy factory owners, while making wage slaves of former artisans by forcing them out of their homes and shops and into dark and dangerous factories, that is, if they were "lucky" enough to have a job at all.

The Luddites did not prevail, of course. Perhaps their battle was hopeless from the start. But at the very least they proved that industrial workers were not as powerless as the wealthy industrialists liked to think they were. Resistance is never futile. We can only imagine what courses of action modern-day Luddites might want to take, and if they would be any more effective than the original tactics, but our consideration of the Luddites should prompt us to ask at least one very important question: Do we believe in progress?

DO YOU BELIEVE IN PROGRESS?

The link between technology and the broader notion of "progress" is a strong one. There is an equally strong, though negative, link between the notion of progress and religion. John Punshon—former English politician, professor of religion, and author of numerous books on Quakerism and Quaker history—told me that he became a committed Christian when he realized he no longer believed in progress. John identified one of the key dialectics in religious thought: whether we should try to engineer our own "salvation," as it were, by creating a better world, a better society, or whether we should depend absolutely on God for any improvement in the human condition. Stated another way, should we put our faith in self-improvement or in God? To a casual observer, the two would not seem to be mutually exclusive, but within Christian theological tradition, where self-reliance is a sin and innovation is a heresy, it is often presented as a stark choice. We should not be surprised, therefore, to find Christian communities antagonistic toward any talk of "progress."

This antagonism is not without merit. At the beginning of the twentieth century, we had high hopes for progress. Improvements in technology, in our understanding of the world around us, and, especially, in our understanding of each other and the human condition all conspired to bring about a better world. It was only a matter of time before most of the problems that plagued human history would be eliminated. Improvements in agriculture would eliminate famine once and for all. Universal education would eliminate ignorance. The increasingly precise science of economics would eliminate poverty, and geometric improvements in manufacturing technology would virtually eliminate material want. Labor-saving devices were popping up in every area of human endeavor, so physical labor would soon be a thing of the past. It seemed the biggest problem we would likely be facing in the twenty-first century would be what to do with all our leisure time!

Most promising perhaps was the emerging so-called social sciences. In the same way that the material sciences improved our control over the natural world, the social sciences would improve our control over our own antisocial behavior. There would be no more wars because there would be no more cause for war. Wars are fought because of competition for scarce resources or because of misunderstanding and fear. With plenty of everything for everybody and with universal understanding and brotherhood, what could we possibly fight about?

It turns out we really didn't need anything to fight about. No one was too sure what we were fighting about in the Great War of 1914–1918. "Making the world safe for democracy" was the best the American president could come up with, but I believe even he knew in his heart of hearts that was nonsense. The war started with an assassination that should have been of little consequence outside a small political circle, but, because of a comedy of diplomatic commitments, a conflagration erupted that would in short order embroil the newfound military might of the entire Western world. From the perspective afforded by history, we refer to this collective insanity as "World War I," as if such hellish acts of global homicide are so routine that we can start numbering them, so it's hard for us to appreciate how shocking this war was to the great thinkers and social scientists of the time. War itself was nothing new, of course, nor were cruelty and brutality, but the sheer scale of human misery and destruction and the cold-blooded mathematical precision with which we could now exterminate each other was literally unprecedented.

There was no reasonable explanation for the Great War. We can reconstruct the now seemingly inevitable events that led to its escalation, but reason had little or nothing to do with all the death and destruction. As the armies faced each other in their trenches, taking turns executing pointless assaults into hails of machine-gun fire and storms of poison gas, no one knew what they were fighting for besides a few acres of ravaged dust or mud; they only knew that "the enemy" was out there and that they must fight. It seemed to many that we were just hell-bent on killing each other, and human progress served mainly to give us more efficient ways of accomplishing just that.

"Progress," it turned out, had less to do with universal understanding and brotherhood than it did with building bigger and better engines of destruction. The only material want the factories seemed to address was for bullets and artillery shells, and though the machines of war turned out corpses in numbers that to this day seem incomprehensible, our old companions disease and famine produced far more.[3]

Later events in the first half of the twentieth century simply drove home the point. No sooner did the Great War end than the seeds of the Second World War began to sprout. Young women and men who witnessed the insanity of the first war would live to fight and die in the second. Those who witnessed the invention of war machines earlier in the century lived to watch newsreels testifying to their perfection. Tanks and machine guns got bigger, faster, more powerful, and more ubiquitous. The airplane that served mainly as a romantic curiosity in the Great War evolved into perhaps the most important strategic tool in our arsenal. The distinction between combatants and civilians, seriously eroded by the end of the century's second decade, all but evaporated by the middle of the fifth. It was now possible, through massive aerial bombardment, to wipe out an entire city in a few minutes, and since it was possible, doing it was inevitable. The association between technology and human misery and destruction on an apocalyptic scale was indelibly etched on our collective soul and can be recalled at any time by uttering one simple word: Hiroshima.

By the end of World War II, the optimism with which we started the century was gone. We still looked to technology to make our lives better, easier, more exciting, but only the very naive could look to it for some kind of salvation from the human condition. The heady, some would even say optimistic, postwar period, culminating in the space race, took on the tone, not of a coming technological utopia, but of a wild party at the end of all things. School children learned how the miracles of science were improving their world while they practiced their "duck and cover" drills. And the doomsday clock ticked on toward midnight.

Today, belief in progress may be staging a comeback, and in many respects the information revolution is the cause. If you read various commentaries on the technology of the day, it's easy to find references to how technology is leveling the playing field and providing unprecedented opportunity and mind-boggling potential for every conceivable good, from improving education and conquering poverty to overcoming disease and even stopping the aging process.

If we are going to understand how we relate to technology as a people of faith, we need to come to terms with how we feel about this whole idea of progress. It may help in that endeavor to take a look at a deeply religious group who is perhaps most closely identified with a strong stand on technology but, in truth, is much more motivated by antagonism toward progress.

AMMANN'S LEGACY

I spend much of my life dealing with things technical. It's a life I've chosen, so I shouldn't really complain, but I do anyway. Sometimes I think I'm ready to sever this relationship, to take a radical stand and swear off nearly every form of modern technology and all it stands for. I'll probably never do it, but here in east-central Indiana I'm literally surrounded by folks who appear to have taken just such a radical stand. I speak, of course, of the Amish. I find the Amish fascinating, and clearly I'm not alone. I'm sure that, like most people, I have a lot of misconceptions about the Amish way of life, but they are clearly a people set apart, and I respect that.

Disengagement from the world is the compelling motivation for the seemingly peculiar behavior of the Amish. There is a strong tendency for spiritual communities to disengage from the outside world. It is an identifying feature of religious cults and it has certainly been the case with Christians, going back to the very early church; according to classic historian Edward Gibbon it was the Christians' perceived antisocial and even misanthropic teachings and behavior that caused them to run afoul of the civic-minded Romans, who were otherwise surprisingly tolerant of and enthusiastic toward foreign religions.[4]

Of course, the very first thing I need to say about the Amish is that there is no "the Amish" in the sense of a monolithic organization with a single set of beliefs, though there are some common features and theological understandings. Certain common (but by no means absolutely uniform) identifying features of Amish life—such as speaking Pennsylvania Dutch (a unique German dialect), wearing "prayer coverings" (white caps or bonnets) or beards without mustaches (mustaches have been associated with the military, so this style of facial hair is common among pacifist groups), "plain" dress (again there is variation here, but to the mainstream twenty-first-century eye it can be hard to tell an Old Order Amish from an Old Order Mennonite from a plain Quaker), using horses for transportation and field work, worship in homes, and rejection of formal education beyond the eighth grade—disguise to the outside world the broad diversity within the Amish order.

The Amish are certainly all Christian in the German Anabaptist tradition, a category that would also include Mennonites and Brethren. In addition to the practice of adult or "believer's" baptism, it's probably fair to say that all German Anabaptists practice some degree of alienation from state and worldly influence, based in part on Paul's various admonitions, including "be not conformed to the world, but be ye transformed by the renewing of your mind, that ye may prove what is that good, and acceptable, and perfect, will of God" (Romans 12:2, KJV).

The Amish are organized into hundreds of congregations in settlements throughout the Americas (most in the United States), and they have a very strong congregational polity, meaning that each congregation is granted autonomy to freely discern the will of God, and therefore the "Ordnung," essentially an unwritten code that guides behavior, for that congregation. Consequently, the behavior that is of greatest interest to this study, namely the Amish use of, or relationship to, technology, varies widely. There are Amish who drive cars and live in houses wired for electricity and telephones. However, when most of us think of the Amish we probably are thinking of Old Order Amish, who generally do not drive cars, have phones, or wire their houses. Yet even among the Old Order Amish there is a great diversity of permitted use and attitudes toward technology. Within a congregation there will be disagreement and debate over the use of a particular technology, so from time to time, generally once or twice per year or as situations or conflicts arise, church leaders gather to discuss issues, including the use of new technologies or new uses of old ones, and may amend the Ordnung for that community accordingly.

My central point is that, contrary to what I used to believe, and what I suspect others may assume as well, the Amish are *not* anti-technology. They are certainly anti-progress in the sense outlined above; that is to say, they find any belief in "the perfectibility of human institutions"[5] to be heretical. But they knowingly embrace any number of technologies, some ancient, some modern. More important to our present study, the Amish have no desire—or if they have the desire they also have enough sense to realize the impossibility—to be frozen in time, saying in effect that eighteenth-century technology is fine but twenty-first-century technology is evil. On the contrary, the Amish have embraced numerous modern technologies to various extents, including (with a lot of variety from community to community) use of cell phones and the Internet,[6] electricity (especially cordless tools), riding in cars and buses, modern farm implements (often horse-drawn), and genetically modified crops.[7]

How an Amish farmer could grow genetically altered crops and order seed on a Blackberry, but refuse to drive a tractor or have electricity or running water in the house, may baffle or even amuse us. But the point is that it makes sense to the farmer and to church leaders. You might be surprised to find the Amish community, in spite of its backward appearance, is growing rapidly, doubling in size approximately every twenty years.[8] Though they claim to welcome converts, the reality is that they attract very few, so their growth is due almost exclusively to a high birth rate (no artificial birth control) and a remarkable ability to retain their young adults.[9] Obviously, if so many young Amish choose to stay Amish, they have something good going. I'm not proposing we consider conversion. I am proposing, however, that we consider *them* and their intentional relationship to technology. We may not want to emulate their theology, but if we can emulate the intentional way they engage technology, considering carefully and thoroughly how it affects us socially and spiritually, we might discover new paradigms for thinking about technology that take us beyond the simplistic Luddite-techtopian dialectic.

As Americans, we are conditioned to accept whatever technology comes along. Sure, as human beings we are resistant to change, but the social and economic pressures to adopt whatever technology is currently being marketed is pretty compelling. Take cable television, for example. Once it was just for people in mountain areas that couldn't get reliable over-the-air reception. The rest of us had to pay for the boob tube itself, and had to put up with approximately eight minutes of commercial interruption per hour in prime time (about half or less than what we put up with now), but otherwise television was free. Now cable service or some variation on it, such as small dish satellite, is considered the norm. People who decide not to shell out upwards of one hundred dollars per month for umpteen channels of commercial-ridden tripe are regarded, especially by their children, as, well, sort of Amish. For most Americans, life without cable television, let alone cars or telephones or computers, would seem nearly impossible, or at least intolerably boring. But would it be, really?

If we are conditioned to accept technology by default, the Amish are conditioned to do exactly the opposite. They carefully and with merited suspicion evaluate every technology in terms of what impact it might have on their way of life. If that impact is positive, they adopt it. If it is negative, the way most Amish congregations have determined having telephones in their homes would be, they reject it. Most Amish will *use* telephones, they just won't have one in their house because it would disrupt the harmony of the home and corrupt their lines of communication, and therefore the structure of their religious order. It's not hypocritical; it's entirely practical and philosophically sound.

It would be hard for one of us to categorically reject a technology. Deciding not to have a phone or a car would present economic hardships for many of us, but the Amish have had a lot of practice at this sort of thing, and have a tight-knit, loving community to support them in their choice. They model a way of encountering technology that would serve all of us well. Rather than blindly accepting new technologies, we could carefully evaluate them in terms of their impact on our desired way of life. To be clear, I'm not suggesting that we adopt Amish theology, spirituality, or values. Our evaluations, and I can hardly emphasize this enough, will have to be made in the context of *our* values and *our* spiritual communities. As with the Amish, different contexts will call for different sets of conclusions.

MOTHER ANN'S GIFT

Our examination of the Luddites reminded us to think critically about progress. Considering the Amish prompted us to question how our beliefs regarding progress might manifest themselves in a philosophy of technology, suggesting that we might be more selective in our use and acceptance of technology. Now we'll turn our attention to the Shakers. Though all three groups bring a high regard for simplicity to bear on their beliefs and practices regarding technology, none does so fully, so unambiguously, or so gracefully as the Shakers.

The Shakers were a utopian Christian American cult founded in the late eighteenth century and effectively extinct by the mid-twentieth. In many respects, they resemble the Amish, particularly with regard to their radical disengagement with the world and their antagonism toward progress. That said, it is a little hard to see exactly where the Shakers fit along the continuum between worldly progress and total disengagement. Indeed, they themselves struggled with this question, and some would claim their partial engagement with the world led to their ultimate decline.[10]

There are also some distinct differences between the Amish and the Shakers; the Shakers being of largely English influence and the Amish of German may well be the least of them. The Shakers' relationship with technology seems rather similar to that of the Amish at first glance. The Shakers were suspicious of technology and, since they embraced an austere life of hard work, could, like the Amish, be expected to reject any technology that claimed to be "labor-saving" or intended to increase creature comfort. Also, like the Amish, the Shakers were suspicious of innovation and had formal procedures for approving the incorporation of a technology into their society.

But though the Amish have embraced various technologies, they are not particularly well known for their engineering skill. On the contrary, the Shakers, ironically, are best known for their contributions to technology, especially their furniture. Granted, most people don't think of furniture as technology, and when describing the contributions of the Shakers, people would most likely speak of "craftsmanship" rather than engineering or technology. But the contributions of the Shakers go well beyond home furnishings, and the Shakers stand out as unique even in an historical period where superb craftsmanship was ubiquitous. They didn't believe in personal property rights, intellectual or otherwise, and wanted to share all their creations freely. Consequently, most of their inventions went unpatented. In spite of this, they filed no fewer than forty patents in the period from 1793 to 1901, proving that they were a highly creative and inventive people.[11]

They clearly set themselves apart, living together in communes, having little contact with the outside world, totally rejecting worldly values to the point of absolute celibacy (which goes a long way toward explaining their ultimate demise), and denying any form of personal enrichment, vowing their total obedience and devotion to God and the community.

They were an extremely industrious and hard-working people, but refused to be paid for their work or even keep track of their hours. Instead, they considered their work to be a spiritual discipline and a gift from God. However, because they had no outside denominational or charitable support, the way a Catholic or Buddhist monastery or other religious commune might typically have, they depended on selling their agricultural and domestic products to the outside world in order to support themselves. As the antebellum American economy became increasingly cash oriented and less barter oriented, the Shakers became increasingly dependent on their business ventures and, therefore, their relations with the outside world.

The Shakers had a unique theological perspective and a unique social order. From a great distance in time and space the Shakers appear quaint and charming, but a closer look reveals a highly developed, intriguing spirituality, as well as a darker side, perhaps best expressed by Charles Dickens, who visited an upstate New York Shaker village in 1842, near the height of their influence. After complimenting the Shakers' kindness, industry, and integrity, he goes on to say,

> I cannot, I confess, incline toward the Shakers; view them with much favor, or extend towards them any very lenient construction. I so abhor, and from my soul detest that bad spirit, by no matter what class or sect it may be entertained, which would strip life of its healthful graces, rob youth of its innocent pleasures, pluck from maturity and age their pleasant adornments, and make existence but a narrow path towards the grave.[12]

I suspect life among the Shakers was not quite as uniformly "grim"—a descriptor he used repeatedly, with comic effect—or as devoid of joy as Dickens perceived from his brief visit to one Shaker community, but there's no question that the

Shakers' deep spirituality was accompanied by, and probably a direct product of, a radical, intense denial of individual identity and total submission to authority. Unlike the Amish, Shakers had a catholic polity, with "all authority [flowing] from a single anointed leader, down through a chain of loyal bishops to the lowliest individual believer."[13]

The Shakers confront us with a bit of a paradox. Their lifestyle, at least when described in the abstract, was so devoid of creature comforts and recreation that few of us would even consider trying to imitate it. Fewer still would be successful. Almost everything about their order would seem to be designed to stifle creativity. Artisans were not allowed to sign their work, nor were they allowed to deviate from proscribed procedures and designs. "Beauty," as they thought of it, was a vanity that had no place in their society. They were strict utilitarians. Knowledge and material goods were valued only so far as they were useful. Leisure was considered an evil and ornamentation was simply not tolerated; it was considered not just useless but actually detrimental to a spiritual lifestyle.

In spite of this, not only did the Shakers contribute countless inventions and technological improvements to the world (they are credited with the invention of the circular saw, to name just one), but their furnishings, tools, and machines are also considered among some of the most beautiful and elegant ever conceived.

> In [Shaker woodworking] certain basic values in the culture found concrete expression; usefulness above all else, no excessiveness in either line or mass, restraint always, strength, proportion—the most assiduous care that the essential function of the piece should be insured. Inspired by and guided by a passionate devotion to the life of the spirit, the society's chair and furniture makers wrought into their work a sincerity freed from all dross

and marked by great humility. In these labors, the artistic coincided with the religious conscience, and in the end we find utilitarianism raised into the realm of undeniable charm and a quiet and pure beauty.[14]

And this is the legacy the Shakers leave us: that when true simplicity, utility, and a heart focused on matters of the spirit (and, quite probably, little else) come together in technology, the result can be charming and beautiful.

I would be even less likely to want to proselytize for the Shakers than I would for the Amish or the Luddites, since I, like Dickens, find much of their philosophy and theology to be downright suffocating. There would be little point anyway, since the Shakers stopped accepting converts some time ago and have since passed into extinction. But couldn't we adopt a sort of "neo-Shaker" attitude toward design and selection of technology, looking for not only a purified utility but also a quiet simplicity and essence?

We, like the Shakers and the Amish, could stand to be more selective in our use of technology, and more practiced in our ability to do without much of what the world tells us is essential—not giving anything up in the sense of a penance, but rather trying to capture some of the underlying motivation for choosing the ascetic life in the first place, letting go of the vanities and ornaments that merely distract us from our true spiritual nature. By so doing, I think we would find a more healthful balance in our lives, where everything we do, including our use of technology, works in harmony with our spiritual ambitions.

The ultimate lesson we can learn from the Shakers, the Amish, and the Luddites, or perhaps it's more of a reminder than a lesson, is that technology exists to serve us, not the other way around. Technology might be the handmaiden of reason, but it should never be our taskmaster, taking us anywhere God has not called us to go.

2

Finding Our Way

I got old just in time.

—Keith Esch, 1998

Keith is a good friend, but also a Luddite, and proud of it. His retirement roughly coincided with my being hired to oversee a grant-funded initiative to drag his beloved seminary, kicking and screaming if necessary, onto the front lines of the information revolution. For better or worse, it was my job to represent the techtopians. Keith, a man of rare wit and wisdom, and now a trustee, which made him my boss's boss, wasn't about to let me off easy.

"I was talking to this friend of mine the other day," Keith told me. "He's been retired for a few years now. 'What are you doing these days?' I asked him. 'Computer,' he says. Now tell me, how can you *do* computer? A computer is *just a tool*, right? I mean, it's like I asked you, 'What are you doing?' and you said 'shovel' or 'hammer.' You can dig a hole or build a house, but if you're just sitting around staring at a shovel or a hammer, that's not *doing* anything."

As is his wont, Keith had cut to the heart of the matter expeditiously and with good humor. Would bringing the information revolution to seminary education really change anything, or was it just a high-tech distraction? Are we really doing anything new with all this technology, or are we just playing around, doing the same old things with some newfangled toys.

JUST A TOOL?

It's a common misconception that tools should just be there for us and that we shouldn't need to spend any time taking care of them or figuring out how to make them work better. On the contrary, all craftsmen (men and women) worth their salt will spend some time selecting and maintaining their tools. There's a good chance that they will even fabricate their own tools, just as many computer "power users" like to build their own computers, sometimes even writing some of their own software. But Keith had a point: we shouldn't have to spend an inordinate amount of time fiddling with our tools. If you had to spend five minutes putting the head back on your hammer every time you drove a nail, you would either start looking around for a better hammer or give up using nails.

The PC (personal computer) is a little like a bad hammer. Anyone who has spent much time using a computer knows that it's easy to get distracted and spend more time figuring out how to do something than you would spend *doing the same thing some other way.* This is not surprising to those of us who started fooling with microcomputers in the late 1970s and spent entire evenings getting them to reproduce a simple pattern on a screen or perform a basic mathematical operation without crashing. They started out as toys for wire heads really, and most of us assumed they would never be much more than that.[1]

Somehow the perception has shifted from PC as high-tech toy to PC as consumer tool, but the device itself has not fundamentally changed that much. Predictably, the hardware has gotten faster and more powerful, the software has gotten much more sophisticated, and developers have tried hard to make computers more "user friendly" (with far too little success). In spite of all that, under the hood the PC itself is pretty much the same ornery anal-retentive beast it always has been, doing precisely what it has been programmed to do, no more, no less, no matter how useless, no matter how far removed from your intentions. That's fine for folks who enjoy fooling around under the hood, but not good news to the vast majority of people out there who just want to get on with their work.

So for better or worse the computer is no longer a toy but has become, instead, a less-than-perfect tool. But is the computer "just a tool," as Keith assumed? Hardly. When people say the computer is "just a tool," they dismiss it too lightly, underestimating its revolutionary potential.[2] Saying the computer is "just a tool" is like saying the atom bomb is "just a tool." True enough, but it doesn't tell the whole story.

For starters, the computer is more like a *toolbox* than a tool. When we speak of "the computer," we are really talking about a whole set of tools, including various peripherals and applications, not just the box itself. If you're like most computer owners, you no doubt have a bunch of tools in there that you don't even know you have, much less how to use them. Not that you should; a lot of the junk shipped with computers and packaged with other software is really third rate, and good craftsmen don't waste time learning how to use lousy tools.

"The computer," as we normally think of it, is a *technology*, not just a tool, and the distinction, if a little nuanced, is extremely important. To put it succinctly: *a technology is a way of using tools to do something.* A new technology usually starts as a way of using new tools to do an old thing, but eventually, a truly new technology (as opposed to the evolution of an old technology) will lead to using new tools to do *new things*. If those new things are sufficiently pervasive, they will eventually change the nature of our society and, in turn, change us and our experience of the world. In other words, *the tools we use and how we use them help to determine how we think, what we believe, and, ultimately, who we are.* I'll outline two historical examples of technologies that have brought about this sort of change. Both are comparable in their own way to computer technology.

HORSELESS CARRIAGES

At one time the automobile was routinely called a "horseless carriage," and prior to the introduction of Ford's Model T the name was entirely apt. The automobile did exactly what the carriage did, less the horse. It even looked a lot like a carriage, and why not? What else would it look like? Like virtually every new technology, automobile technology simply did some old thing (riding around town) a new way. Proponents of the new technology talked about its advantages (less attitude and lower maintenance) and downplayed the disadvantages, while detractors pointed out the advantage of the old technology (horses rarely burst into flames and arguably smelled better). Over time, the technology improved to the point where it dominated and was adopted by the majority; buggy-whip makers went broke while gasoline refiners got rich. Same old story so far: new technology replaces old technology, some prosper, some don't, and life goes on much as before.

But then something started to happen. Gradually we started to change the way we thought about transportation. Cars (we stopped thinking of them as horseless carriages) went faster and farther than we could ever go using horses, and, encouraged by the advertising industry, we started to think of them as extensions of ourselves in some way. The car we drove, which was starting to look a lot less like a carriage, said something about who we were; we have a *relationship* with our car that is much different than the relationship we might have with a horse. Meanwhile, tire and automobile manufacturers, oil companies, construction interests, and governments conspired to build highway systems the likes of which were previously *unimaginable,* and that's a key word; a new technology often opens up the imagination to *new* (not necessarily *good*) ideas.

By the 1960s, automobile technology had completely transformed our society. We now were much more likely to live far away from where we worked. Suburban sprawl, malls, and parking lots galore were the inevitable byproducts. Here in the United States there is hardly an aspect of modern life that hasn't been impacted in a major way by the automobile. Even our churches and synagogues have changed; many old "neighborhood" churches have virtually no members living in the neighborhood anymore, and many more have had to move into newer buildings not because the old ones weren't big enough, but because they couldn't procure enough parking at their old locations.

Sure, the central doctrines and creeds of a given religion probably won't change as a *direct* result of the automobile, but the automobile has certainly affected approaches to evangelism, and such massive fundamental changes in the nature and makeup of the congregation can't help but change the worship experience, and consequently the spirituality of the congregants. The modern megachurch with its five-figure membership rolls would be untenable, and unimaginable, without the automobile or something very much like it, and I have little doubt that such churches are influencing Christian theology, especially as it is perceived by the broader public.

But aside from the ecclesiological impact of the automobile, imagine having to depend on a living, breathing creature for your transportation needs. While you're at it, imagine spending an hour or more every day walking and spending most of your days within a few miles of where you woke up. Do you think your spiritual life would look different, living in such a world, than it does today?

THE GUTENBERG GALAXY

Another example of a technology that has transformed our world is typography, traditionally attributed to Johannes Gutenberg, though he invented neither the printing press nor movable type. We like to simplify things and attribute new technologies to a single tool or inventor, but the real story is always more complex and more interesting. In this case, Gutenberg came up with a process for producing high-quality movable type, which coincided with the development of the printing press, new techniques and economies for cheaply producing mass quantities of paper, and a simple alphabet and punctuation set. The combination sparked a cultural revolution that changed our world so fundamentally that it's nearly impossible for us to conceive of what it was previously like.

Saying that the Gutenberg Bible transformed the world is a gross simplification of history, but in a mythological sense it's true nonetheless. Prior to this technology, knowledge was transmitted and preserved primarily through oral tradition. Written languages had been around for millennia and had a significant impact on our culture, but literacy rates were low and written materials rare, precious, and mostly ancient. Suddenly all that changed, and the written word went from being a tool for elite scholars and historians to a tool for mass communication. That's clear enough now to our post-Gutenberg mind-set, but prior to the fifteenth century there was really no such thing as mass communication as we think of it.

With the advent of modern printing, suddenly Bibles— including, eventually, common language translations—and other books were everywhere. Literacy became a matter of religious obligation. At first the new technology was seen as just a way to do some old thing (produce books) in a more efficient way, but soon people, most notably Martin Luther and other leaders of the Reformation, started using the technology to do a very new thing, even if they weren't aware that what they were doing was revolutionary.

Pre-Gutenberg, a person could express an idea verbally, perhaps even to a large crowd, and that idea might catch on and spread, passed by "word of mouth." But post-Gutenberg, a person, such as Luther, could write down that idea, laying arguments out carefully and logically, and within weeks it might be spread, *preserved in all its detail,* on a continental scale. Politically and/or religiously charged commentaries could be quickly printed onto tracts and distributed widely to an increasingly literate populace, sometimes to great and immediate effect.

Of course, we all know that the revolution Gutenberg sparked played a central role in the Protestant Reformation, as well as in various other efforts at reform within the Catholic Church (sometimes referred to as the Counter Reformation) and the rise of most of the so-called "traditional" churches of our day. But the most profound effect of the Gutenberg revolution was so subtle we can only be aware of it through the perspective of history. What many people don't—and what Martin Luther and his contemporaries couldn't—appreciate is how typography and paper affected how we acquire, evaluate, and perceive the limits of knowledge, our *epistemology.* Pre-Gutenberg, people believed what they *heard;* post-Gutenberg they believed what they *read.* And hearing is different than reading; the written word is fundamentally different than the spoken word. The preeminence of the written word has changed the way we think and reason; indeed reason and logic themselves are consequences of our reliance on the written word to arbitrate truth.[3]

SAVE EVERYTHING, FIND ANYTHING

What the automobile, the printing press, and every other revolutionary technology have in common is that they all started out as simple tools, conceived to fill a perceived and extant need, and eventually evolved into technologies that had us doing things that were, if not completely different, at least conceptually unprecedented. Though the revolutionary potential of the computer has been apparent to many since its conception, it remains to be seen just how far the revolution will go. It might be an exaggeration to say that, as a technology, computers are in their infancy; the programmable electronic computer has been with us for a little over half a century and the PC—which I'll say was born in 1984 when the Macintosh was introduced, though others might date it a little earlier—about half as long. But as technologies evolve that's still pretty young, say, preadolescent.

We're essentially at the stage Martin Luther and his contemporaries were with typography; we may sense that we've already stepped over the threshold of something big, something transformative, but we lack the perspective of history to truly understand how far we have come, or how deep the rabbit hole might go. Today we mostly use computers to do things we could do, perhaps even used to do, some other way. Most of us use them as glorified typewriters. Sure, we do things with computers we might not do otherwise, mostly because we wouldn't have the time or it wouldn't seem like as much fun, but we *could,* if we chose to, do them some other way. We write e-mails instead of letters, use Quicken or Microsoft Money instead of handwritten ledgers to manage our finances, use digital rather than film photography, and so on. The fact that we still use the same words, like *photograph, e-mail,* spread*sheets,* to describe these activities points to their pre-digital antecedents. But what are we doing with computers that's truly new? Where is this revolution I keep talking about?

As I've already said, that remains to be seen. But I believe that, like typography, the computer could ultimately change everything, but perhaps most significantly it will change our epistemology, including how we acquire, evaluate, and perceive our spiritual beliefs. In other words, the computer will change not just how we evaluate facts but also how we understand *truth,* and therefore how we understand *God.*

The revolution has begun. No one knows for sure where it will take us, but it's not too early to start trying to find out. How is computer technology beginning to affect our epistemology?

It's all about data. Computers do a lousy job of dealing with people, but they do an absolutely amazing job of dealing with numbers—not surprising, as that's what they were invented to do. When we let numbers stand for other things— for example, every punctuation mark and letter of the alphabet has a corresponding representative number inside your computer—we call it "data," and even the most rudimentary computers can handle data with a speed and deftness that no human being could begin to imitate. In the early years of computer science, speed and accuracy were the main factors; at first we started using computers for things we wouldn't do otherwise because it would take too long, because it would cost too much, or because we would probably make some minor error that would goof up our results anyway—an error that would be literally impossible for a computer to make. Later we used computers for things we truly *couldn't* do without them because we simply wouldn't live long enough to see the results. Consequently, computers have truly revolutionized the sciences; we can now make mathematical models and perform experiments in cyberspace that would be impossible in physical space.

It has taken a while for data storage technology to catch up with advances in data processing technology, but we've now arrived at the point where we can save huge amounts of data very inexpensively. Indeed, the current deflation rate in data storage costs now dwarfs the otherwise impressive plunge in processing costs. The breakthrough "ah-hah" moment came for me when I heard someone on the radio say that it now costs more to throw data away than it does to keep it. Think about that for a moment. Have you ever tried to tidy up the files on your computer? Think of how long it takes to open a file up, confirm what's in it, make a value judgment, and then delete it. Multiply that by the thousands or even millions of files in enterprise-scale data systems and you begin to see the hopelessness of the task.

Now think of your local library. Like all libraries, it has limited resources and limited shelf space, so it needs to be selective about which works it acquires and it needs to cull its holdings from time to time in order to make room for new acquisitions. Now consider that all the text in all the books and magazines in your local library could be "digitized" (converted to numbers, essentially), stored on computer media, and take up less space than your coffee table. What incentive would librarians have to cull their holdings under those circumstances?

But how do we make sense of all that data? The situation is similar in the physical world. I'm a chronic DIYer (do-it-yourselfer), so I keep a lot of resources (junk) around my shop. Like the local librarian, I have limited space, but the real challenge is not finding room for all the stuff; the real challenge is being able to find what I want, or even remembering that I have it in the first place. Have you ever run out and bought some doodad, only to later discover the same item where you had tucked it away, just in case you ever needed it? In the digital world we have the same problem in spades. Given a vast, literally incomprehensible amount of data, how do you even know what you have, let alone find what you need?

There are two basic approaches to the problem: create an organizational structure or come up with a clever search strategy. Both are useful, usually necessary, and ideally suited to computer-mediated approaches. Fortunately, both also have their physical-world counterparts, so it should be fairly easy to explain, with a grossly simplified analogy, how each works.

In my shop, I try to organize my junk, er, resources, into some kind of logical structure, keeping similar items together—tools in one area and supplies in another, spare parts in yet another—and creating nested hierarchies, like supplies/plumbing/fittings/plastic. These are all *structural* strategies—trying to create some type of cognitive organizational map for what's tucked away in various drawers, shelves, and cabinets.

It's an imperfect science, of course, and I'm constantly struggling with items that seem to cross or defy categories; does the 10W-40 oil go with the lubricants or the automotive supplies? Do I put the nails for my nail guns with the tools where the nail guns are, or in supplies/fasteners/nails/nail gun with the regular nails? Libraries use much more developed and sophisticated structural approaches to organize their holdings, including, probably, something like the Dewey decimal system or Library of Congress catalog numbers, but they face many of the same basic dilemmas I do in organizing my junk.

In a very similar way, computer data can be (and in most cases needs to be) structured. One structural approach you probably use on your computer is to organize your data files into various directories or "folders" and sub-directories. This type of structure is pretty similar, conceptually, to the one I use in my shop. Another approach is to store data in a *database,* which is much more comparable to one of the more sophisticated approaches used by your libraries. Structuring data and designing a database in which to store it is a little like playing the violin. It's easy to do (just scratch the bow across the strings with one hand and wiggle your fingers on the strings with the other; what's the big deal?), but hard to do well. That said, once you conceive of a structural system for your data, implementing it is a breeze; computers can move huge amounts of data around in a snap. Implementing a new organizational system in my shop could take weeks, and imagine how long it would take to re-stack the entire holdings of your library.

Having your junk/books/data organized into a well-designed, logical structure makes it a lot easier to know what you have, but you still need a search strategy to find what you are looking for. The obvious prerevolutionary strategy is to become familiar with the organizational structure, predict where an item fits into the structure, and look for it there. That's the search strategy I use in the shop. I use labels and other visual clues that roughly parallel the organizational struc-ture I've attempted to impose on all the piles of junk. When I need something I use these clues and, with luck and persistence, sometimes find what I'm looking for.

In the library we might use a similar search strategy if we're pretty familiar with the library's structural strategy, or if we're just browsing, but more likely we'll use the "card cata-log." Up until about 1990 or so, the card catalog was probably just that: a bunch of drawers with thousands of little cards in them, each card corresponding to a holding in the library. (I use one of these old card catalog cabinets to store junk in my shop. Ironic, huh?)

A computer can do a much better job of effectively rifling through thousands of those little cards than you or I ever could, and nowadays most large libraries have replaced their old card catalogs with computer-based search systems. Some of the early systems libraries used were absolutely dreadful, and prime examples of just how badly you can screw things up with a computer, but fortunately well-designed and easy-to-use computer-based "card catalogs" (we're only gradually drop-ping that name as a generation of students who have never seen the real thing graduate from college) are now the norm.

But notice I said that computers can rifle through those cards faster than we can. Sure, it's an example of how computers can do something *better,* but have they done anything that's really *different?* In some respects no, but sometimes they can do something so much better that it causes a true paradigm shift, much the way the automobile took over the role of the horse, yet managed to transform the way we think about not only transportation but also time, space, location, community, work, home, and even our own identity. The fact that computer technology can preserve data so much more efficiently than typography implies that perhaps we really can "save everything." True, we can't save an infinite amount of data, but we can't produce an infinite amount of data either, and so far we're getting better at saving data faster than we are getting better at producing it, so essentially, we soon will be able to save everything. For my money, that's an extraordinarily mind-bending concept. But even if we flip through those cards really really fast, can we truly "find anything"?

To find an example of something being done so much better that it ends up being something truly different, something that actually changes the way we *think,* we need look no further than the World Wide Web. No, we're not going to find it on some pundit's blog, but rather in the way we search the Web itself.

If we think of the Web as a big library, it is pretty much the Wild West out there; there's no librarian shushing anybody or charging overdue fines, and there's certainly no one culling the Web's "holdings"; anybody, and I mean absolutely *anybody,* can add to the Web's holdings by simply posting a new website, and if you've spent any time at all "surfing" you know there are no quality standards and effectively no editorial controls, let alone censorship. There's gold in them-thar hills, but you have to dig through a lot of mud to find it.

There is indeed some limited organizational structure to the Web, though it's not always obvious. If you have a good idea what you are looking for and where you're likely to find it—such as product information on a specific manufacturer's site or a form or brochure from a government site—you can depend upon this structure. But unlike the Dewey decimal or Library of Congress system, the Web's organizational structure is essentially useless if you're just trolling for information on a specific topic.

Yet the Web is extremely searchable thanks to the fact that a lot of really smart people have been working on the problem for a long time and just keep getting better and better at it. I wish I could explain to you how Google and some of the other so-called "search engines" really work, but to do that I would have to be privy to some pretty tightly held trade secrets. I would also have to be a lot smarter. But even if I took a stab at it I would be off on a tangent really. Suffice it to say that the search strategies employed are highly sophisticated, highly eso-teric, highly algorithmic, and only possible using bank upon bank of interconnected high-speed computers. And here's the kicker: *the search strategies used by Google (and others) are truly new things, things we not only couldn't do before we had computers but also things we truly never would have thought to try before.*

Sometimes you will hear people refer to the information revolution as the information *explosion,* referring to how much more we could read/watch/listen to if we chose to, implying that there is much more than we could possibly process. True, but is that really much different than before? Our grandparents probably had more books available to them in their local libraries than they could ever read in a lifetime, so how truly revolutionary is it to have a hundred or a million or a billion times more than you could read in a lifetime? We had three tel-evision channels to choose from when I grew up. Now my par-ents have about a hundred, but they still only watch one at any given time, and, like everybody else it seems, they still com-plain about the lack of quality programming. The song "57

Channels (And Nothin' On)"[4] may sum up our cynical reaction to this "information explosion," but it is hardly the anthem to a revolution.

What is revolutionary is the way we restore and retrieve information, the way we sift through and make some sense of the otherwise hopelessly immense quantity of data we are amassing. "Data mining" is in the news a lot as I write, mostly within the context of national security versus privacy issues (a false dichotomy by the way; well-designed security measures invade privacy minimally, if at all).[5] Data mining may not be an entirely new concept, but emerging data storage, data structuring, and, especially, data search technologies take it to a new level, making it so different than anything that could be contemplated using old technology that it truly is an entirely new critter.

We are fast approaching a world where we can save everything and be able to find anything. And that, it seems to me, can't help but change the way we think over time—how we define and evaluate knowledge, what it means to be smart, and how we value information. Already people are beginning to wonder how we define intelligence in a world where any computer-literate person with a network connection and a Web browser can access, at least potentially, virtually all the knowledge in the world. What good is encyclopedic knowledge when the world's largest, most exhaustive, truly unabridged encyclopedia can be carried in your briefcase? The question becomes even more relevant when we extrapolate only slightly on current technology to imagine a biologically implanted Internet appliance, a prosthesis for the brain, if you will.

And what difference does it make whether something is "published" or not if everything ever written by anybody, from Shakespeare to your nephew's book report, is the same number of clicks away. Let me be clear, I'm not saying that in the post-information-revolution era Shakespeare and your nephew's book report will hold the same *value*, I'm merely saying that they will share the same *accessibility,* and therefore our *value system* must and will change. And if our intellectual value system changes, how can our spirituality, our ways of experiencing and thinking about the Divine, possibly stay the same?

Ready or not, the revolution is upon us.

3

VIRTUAL VILLAGE

*Not only is distance annihilated, but when, as now, the loco-
motion and the steamboat, like enormous shuttles, shoot every
day across the thousand various threads of national descent
and employment, and bind them fast in one web, an hourly
assimilation goes forward and there is no danger that local
peculiarities and hostilities should be preserved.*

—Ralph Waldo Emerson, 1844[1]

Perhaps you've heard that religion is the second most popular
use of the Internet. The first, of course, is pornography. Such
statistics have all the trappings of urban legend, including a lack
of the sort of specificity required to make them truly meaningful. (What do you mean by "popular" and how do you measure it? Who's doing the measuring and how are they doing it?
How do you define *religion* or *pornography*, or do you just
know it when you see it?) Legend or not, this oft-quoted "sta-
tistic" does point to an undeniable truth: both pornography

and religion have flourished on the Internet. Why is that? Is it merely an ironic coincidence?

Hardly. The Internet offers variety (whatever you're into, you're sure to find it), privacy (with minimal care no one needs to know what you are up to), and anonymity (no one needs to know who you really are; you can even pretend to be someone else). These are obvious attractions to consumers of pornography, but it doesn't take a lot of imagination to see how spiritual "seekers" would flock to the Internet as well. Anyone shopping for a religion[2] will find them all on the Web—even the Amish—and can *safely* investigate them. Perhaps it is the relative safety of the Internet—the appearance, at least,[3] of privacy and anonymity—more than anything else that has led to the rise of religion on the Web.

But the Web offers much more than just a safe place for religious tourists, and not everybody practicing religion on the Web is a "seeker"; many are finders, and what they have found is, if not a new set of religious beliefs, at least a new way of religious practice. And while the relative safety of the Web may lend itself to individuals seeking to refine and better understand and interpret their religious belief system or *theology* (though certainly not all religious people are theists, particularly on the Web), religious expression, *spirituality,* is a much more overtly corporate enterprise.

Increasingly the Web is not seen just as a way for the individual to access vast quantities of data, as in the lone religious seeker looking for truth out there somewhere, but also as a way for people to come together, to *be* together, in cyberspace. But is being together in cyberspace the same as being together in physical space? Of course not, but the differences are not as stark or as clear as you might think. Just how is the information revolution changing our experience of community? That's the question with which we'll wrestle for the remainder of this chapter.

COMMUNITIES IN CYBERSPACE

We may consider our spirituality something that is deeply personal and internal, but a healthy spirituality usually has some form of outward expression in a faith community. Or perhaps I have it exactly backwards; perhaps our spirituality comes out of the community and finds its expression internally in our hearts and minds. Perhaps it's a little of both. Regardless, true community, or what many people call "a sense of community," is something the human heart longs for and something that a lot of us seem to feel missing in some measure from our modern life.[4]

Community is a word that suffers from overuse. It has been applied so liberally to nearly any group of people (and occasionally even animals) with any perceivable common feature, let alone affiliation, that most of us barely bat an eye at such absurdities as "the coffee drinking community" or even "the pedestrian community." Indeed, the word *community* has become so tractable as to have become essentially meaningless.[5]

That's a shame because it's a perfectly good word. I would like to try to rescue it, if only for the sake of our discussion, by borrowing a fairly strict definition of community from George Wood, an educator and leading expert on community education. According to Dr. Wood a true community is

> a group of people who have a sense of common purpose(s) and/or interest(s) for which they assume mutual responsibility, acknowledge their interconnectedness, respect the individual differences among members, and commit themselves to the well-being of each other and the integrity and well-being of the group.[6]

Even with this strict definition of community, it's worth reminding ourselves that what is called a community by one person may just look like an organization, an institution, a clique, a gang, or a club to someone else—even someone supposedly included in the so-called community. Which is not to say that a gang, for example, couldn't be a community; it's just to point out that true community, or what might be better called a *sense of community*, is not determined by outward social structures, but rather by the inward feelings and motivations of the members.

Using Wood's definition of community, two other factors immediately come to the forefront. First, we are likely to belong to several communities simultaneously, and we are likely to enter into and leave scores of communities over the course of our lifetimes. This is in sharp contrast to the traditional notion that we belong to one specific community, perhaps even considering that community "home" long after we have ceased to live there. In this respect the modern perception of community, even true community, has changed from what it used to be—due in no small part to the automobile, the telephone, and various other technological developments—and will continue to evolve as new technologies come along.

Second, community is not necessarily defined by political or geographic boundaries, by *place* in other words. This in itself is not an innovation; the traditional use of the word includes communities not defined by borders, a classic example being the post-Diaspora "Jewish community." Communities that *are* defined by place make up a special category that Wood calls "geopolitical communities."

So if communities are not defined by geopolitical boundaries, it is certainly possible for there to be communities in cyberspace, sometimes referred to as "virtual communities." But before we start talking about virtual communities or communities in cyberspace, it's worth exploring what we mean by the terms *virtual* and *cyberspace*. These popular terms are used somewhat interchangeably, and both have been necessary to fill a void in our vocabulary, a void created by the rise in popularity of personal computing and the Internet. That said, I would argue that both terms are reaching the end of their usefulness and that in order for us to better understand the current state of technology and how it affects us spiritually we need to start trying to move beyond them.

WHERE'S CYBERSPACE?

The term *cyberspace* is thought to have been coined by science fiction author William Gibson in his 1984 novel *Neuromancer*. It quickly entered the language as a word to describe the "place" where people go when they go online. It is a cognitive construct, like all words I suppose, but a very conscious one. When people "go" online—when they use a computer and the Internet to interact with other people, such as when they send an e-mail or "enter" a chat "room," and/or to interact with other computers, such as when they "visit" a Web "site"—we say that they are "moving" about in cyberspace. Note that in the previous sentence I placed in quotation marks all the words that would normally be used in conjunction with physical space. *Going, visiting, entering,* and *moving* are all verbs that imply location or movement in physical space; *room* and *site* are nouns that denote specific locations in physical space. It is more than mere convenience that we use these verbs and nouns; it would be nearly impossible to talk about "navigating" the Internet without invoking the metaphor of space.

We might want to say that cyberspace is an imaginary place. But anyone who has spent a little time in cyberspace knows that what you find there is not imaginary. Cyberspace may not be physical space, but it is very real. Our experiences using computers and the Internet are equally real, as are the people we meet online.

When we meet people in cyberspace, we really do meet them, even though we would normally associate the word *meeting* with an event taking place in physical space. Granted, we can't reach out and grasp their hand; we can't smell their cologne (though a technology that would allow that is easy to conceive). We might not immediately learn their gender, race, approximate age, or physical deformities (things we'd like to believe wouldn't affect our reactions appreciably) the way we would if we met them in physical space, but we have met them just the same.

The problem with using the word *cyberspace* is that it suggests an unreality or some *imaginary* domain where we congregate. I'm not saying that cyberspace is a bad word or that we shouldn't use it; what I'm suggesting is that what we've been calling cyberspace for a score or so of years now is so ubiquitous and so much a part of the world around us that we should stop thinking of it as anything "other" than the "real world." Instead of calling it cyberspace, how about we just call it "the world."[7]

When we engage each other via the Internet (or using similar technology by some other means) the experience is *mediated* by the technology. Computer-mediated communication is evolving rapidly, to the point where calling it "communication" is misleading. Communication suggests passing words back and forth, like what you do via correspondence or the telephone. But in our computer-mediated interactions with each other we are more and more inclined to think of ourselves as *being* with rather than just *communicating* with each other. I speak in generalities of course, and if you're new to computer-mediated interactions you probably don't feel this way at all; chances are you find the computer a little obstructive, much the way a previous generation probably found the telephone at first. The computer gets in the way of a natural exchange of ideas and emotions. With time and experience this feeling fades, though, and as the technology evolves, and as a generation grows up with it, using a computer to be with your friends will become as natural and transparent as breathing.

VIRTUAL COMMUNITY

Unlike *cyberspace,* the word *virtual* has been with us for a long time, more than six hundred years according to my dictionary. It means having the same or nearly the same effect as something without actually being that thing. So if I said "this [expletive deleted] computer is virtually useless," I mean that the computer in question is still technically working, but I don't anticipate getting any use out of it in the immediate future, hence it has the effect of being useless even though it really isn't. I also use the word, incorrectly I suppose, as a bit of hyperbole, where it becomes a synonym for *nearly*, as in the above example: the computer isn't *completely* useless—it makes a dandy doorstop.

It's easy to see how the word *virtual* became associated with computers. Computers do a swell job of processing mathematical models of the real world; it was and still is one of their primary applications, particularly in the sciences. As computers have become more powerful and have gotten better at this sort of thing, and especially as devices have been developed that can create a realistic sensory-oriented interface between the computer and its operator—such as high-fidelity sound, enhanced high-definition graphics, and various strategies for detecting and simulating movement and touch—the notion of "virtual reality," or VR, came into being. A flight simulator is a type of VR. Flight simulators can be very rudimentary and primitive, such as the home PC versions that are widely and inexpensively available, or extremely sophisticated, where the pilot experiences a simulation so realistic that it qualifies as flight time for FAA (Federal Aviation Administration) training requirements.

VR is pretty innocuous in its present state but is potentially quite subversive. One of the first applications of VR I ever

saw was a CAD (computer assisted design) system where people wearing high definition video goggles and a few sensors
attached to their body could "walk" through their new home
before a single brick was laid or nail driven, moving windows
and doors around, enlarging or eliminating them at will, raising
the ceiling or pushing out a wall with the wave of a hand. The
changes thus made were recorded and reflected in the design
documentation the builders used to construct the "real" version. It should be obvious how useful such a system could be to
architects and designers, but it is perhaps equally obvious how
such a technology, sufficiently advanced, might impart godlike
power to alter our reality. Of course all this is irresistible fod-
der for science fiction authors and raises fundamental questions
about the nature of reality, such as:

> What is real? How do you define real? If you're talking
> about what you can feel, what you can smell, what you
> can taste and see, then real is just electrical signals,
> interpreted by your brain.[8]

The questions sound rhetorical. It's asked of Neo by
Morpheus, two of the three central characters in the movie *The
Matrix*. The movie takes place in the future where humans have
lost a cataclysmic war against technology and now live inside
an artificial reality created for them by a vast computer network. It's a comic book scenario, with several improbable, if
not impossible, presumptions, so we needn't take the movie
seriously as a cautionary tale on the order of *1984* or *Dr.
Strangelove*, but it does pose serious philosophical questions.[9]
Morpheus is driven to remove himself and others from the
computer-generated reality so that they can live in what he himself calls the "real world," so clearly he is not done wrestling with
the question he seems to answer, though only conditionally. But
if he's right, if real is what is happening in your brain, then the

only thing "virtual" about VR is that the technology isn't good enough yet. Once we have the technology to completely fool our senses, then computer-generated constructs will be, by definition, real; at which point it won't really be "fooling" anyone, will it? At that point, a point not very far off in my humble opinion, VR technology will be doing nothing less than enabling us to experience an *alternate*, not a virtual, reality.

It's a reality that the computers (or, arguably, their programmers) will have created, to be sure. In terms of "real" space, it exists only in the circuits of the computer, but in terms of our *experience* of reality—and ultimately what else do we have?—there will be nothing *virtual* about it. It may be sufficiently different (suspension or modification of certain laws of physics possibly) that we could distinguish it from what we now, comfortably, consider reality, at which point we'd have to decide what to call it. Will we have created a new universe where the laws of physics are different? Or will we have just crossed over into a universe that already existed?[10] Whatever we call this reality, it wouldn't be appropriate to call it "virtual" anymore, at least not until we come up with a different answer to Morpheus's initial questions: What is real? How do you define real?

For the time being, there is a clear difference between the reality generated by a computer and unmediated reality, but that clarity is fading fast. I'm not suggesting that the differences will ever disappear, or be insignificant, just that they won't be so clear, and that the term *virtual* will not become the best way to describe them.

We need not go too much further down this road right now, though we'll revisit the neighborhood a bit in chapter 5 when we cover artificial intelligence. Suffice it to say that VR is a fascinating concept, wrought with potential practical, social, and philosophical implications. But has the whole idea been overplayed a bit? Escaping reality by entering into another "artificial" reality is nothing new. Isn't that what you are doing when you read a great novel or have a particularly vivid dream?

The differences are primarily matters of degree and familiarity; *degree* in that novels rely primarily on our imagination with minimal sensory engagement, while VR, at the theoretical extreme, totally dominates all our senses; *familiarity* in that we're used to reading and dreaming, so those activities don't frighten us as much as the prospect of Matrix-like VR might, nor are they as likely to make us ask the same sort of fundamental epistemological questions, even though those questions are age-old. The cognitive dissonance experienced by Neo upon learning that he has been living his whole life inside a computer program is not unlike that posited by René Descartes nearly four hundred years ago.[11]

The problem with the word *virtual* is that, much like the word *community*, it has been overused to the point where it has lost a lot of its meaning. Nowadays, anything remotely related to a computer gets labeled "virtual"; we read "virtual books," take "virtual meetings," work in "virtual offices," attend "virtual churches." What's next? A "virtual god"? The thing that really put me over the edge is when distance educators started using phrases like "virtual classrooms," "virtual education," and even "virtual learning." Virtual learning is what I would be trying to make happen if I simulated a life form within a computer program and then attempted to teach it something. Is that what they're trying to do?

There is a place for the term *virtual* in the computer world; for example, you have "virtual memory" inside your computer. It serves the same purpose as real memory. Actually it's much slower, but it keeps your computer from just giving up and crashing when it runs out of real memory. It isn't really memory, and internally it works much differently than real memory does, but it has nearly the same effect, so we call it virtual memory.

The term is completely appropriate and even helps you to understand a little better how your computer works.

The same cannot be said of most of the things the word *virtual* gets applied to. Instead it creates an often meaningless distinction between something done with a computer and a similar thing done some other way. "Virtual" implies "fake" in a way that just doesn't fit with the technology; it imposes an artificial unreality, if you will. It's as if by applying the modifier "virtual" to something, we can take it less seriously, consider it less valuable, or somehow compromised, because it isn't the *real* thing after all, it's only the *virtual* thing. Hogwash. It may well be less valuable, compromised, or less worthy of serious consideration, but if so let us make that judgment case by case on the merits, not by way of linguistic prejudice.

So let's drop this horrible idea of a "virtual" community. When people, *real* people, communicate with each other, are *with* each other in a computer-mediated environment, they form real communities, communities where they share a common purpose or interest—often spiritual purposes or interests— for which they assume mutual responsibility, acknowledge their interconnectedness, respect the individual differences among members, and commit themselves to the well-being of each other and the integrity and well-being of the group.

My experience helping to build and foster distance learning communities leads me to believe that the less *virtual* they try to be, the more success they will have.[12] Early attempts at creating virtual environments that were imitations of their "real world" counterparts were dismal failures, in my humble opinion; "virtual classrooms" may be cute, and may seem like a good idea to the unimaginative, but students and teachers don't need pale imitations of brick and mortar institutional trappings; they need rich environments where they can excel. Creating those environments online takes experience, skill, patience, creativity, and a lot of goodwill on everyone's part. A little luck doesn't hurt either, nor does a little help from God.

Creating strong spiritual communities online probably requires the same mixture. Computer-mediated learning employs different strategies on the part of both teachers and students, but learning is learning. Computer-mediated learning may have some limitations and may be different than its counterpart in the classroom, but it can be effective and powerful in ways that a classroom cannot, and classrooms come with their own limitations. Certainly the same could be said for computer-mediated spirituality. Like online learning communities, online spiritual communities are bound to look a little different than what we're used to, but they are no less real.

ANNIHILATING TIME AND SPACE

Until the early nineteenth century, communication and transportation technologies were largely unchanged from their Iron Age antecedents, at least in terms of speed; people, goods, and messages moved along pretty much at walking speed, either human or horse. With the advent of the steamship, the locomotive, and the telegraph, all that changed, and the effect was dizzying. People who saw an approaching train for the first time sometimes thought it was getting physically larger because they had never seen a change in perspective demonstrated at such incomprehensible speed—a speed few of us would be content to drive any longer than it took us to get out of the parking lot. By compressing the time it took for words and objects to get from point A to point B, technology was bringing points A and B effectively closer and closer together, making our world smaller; according to the stock phrase of that day, technology was "annihilating time and space."[13]

The information revolution has taken the "annihilation of time and space" to another level. The gradual devirtualization (to coin a phrase) of virtual reality, which I have described, is one way *space* is being annihilated. On a much more mundane level, the way we are beginning to communicate on the Internet could be thought of as an attempt to annihilate *time*.

In a "normal" conversation, both parties occupy the same space (well not *literally,* but you know what I mean*)* at the same time. We call this *synchronous* (same-time) communication. A telephone conversation is synchronous communication; both parties are occupying the same time frame, but they are not in the same place, so it's *aconcomitant* (not-same-place). We have *virtually* annihilated space (the two parties are really far apart in space, but it rarely matters how far, so space is of no consequence) but not time. A chat room is another place where synchronous aconcomitant exchanges take place.

But there are situations where synchronous aconcomitant communication doesn't work well, where time is a problem. Say you want to chat with your good friend, but you're in New York and your friend is in Sydney. Due to the pesky mechanics of the solar system, just about the time you feel like sitting down for a chat, your friend is probably looking forward to a few more hours of sleep before getting up and going to work. Different personal schedules and preferences can create a similar situation even in the same time zone. What can you do in this situation?

You send an e-mail, of course. Your friend gets up, reads your e-mail, perhaps sending off a quick reply. You read the reply at your convenience, post a reply of your own, and so it goes. It's chat, of a sort, but it's *asynchronous* chat. Threaded discussion boards (essentially websites where various e-mail-like messages on a given topic are displayed together contextually), blogs (Web-based journals/logs), or even social networking schemes like MySpace are technologically enhanced examples of the same principle. They offer a plethora of organizing and content tools, allow for additional participants in various social situations, and impart a variety of possible tones and flavors to the mix.

We haven't truly annihilated time any more than the locomotive or the telegraph did, but like those technologies some of the Internet tools we're using mess with our perception of time and its consequences. In online environments people can share their thoughts and feelings, sometimes more completely and with more freedom than they could in face-to-face situations. In a cold, literal sense, in terms of its brute technology, the Internet is just fast letter-writing, something we've been doing since before the time of Saint Paul. But because it's so much faster and easier, and because of all the organizational and content-oriented enhancements, it changes the way we think about time and space and how we use both to build community.

GLOBAL VILLAGE

Our world today is not only smaller than what it was when we were born, but it's also flatter: flat as in "a level playing field," that is. The information revolution promises, much like Samuel Colt's revolver, to be the great equalizer, and on a global scale. Sooner or later Europeans and Americans will have to face the reality that kids born into so-called Third World countries can grow up just as smart as their kids, and are more and more likely to be competing with their kids for the twenty-first-century equivalent of the corner office.[14]

So will the information revolution have us assimilated into one huge global village? Not likely, though we have some cause to fear that, given the cultural homogenization and loss of "local peculiarities" we have witnessed since Emerson wrote the piece that opened this chapter. The thing that really struck me about that quotation is that Emerson saw national assimilation as a *positive* force. We would do well to remember that attitude as we long for the "good old days" of town squares and tight-knit geopolitical communities. Colloquialism has a dark side, and I imagine that growing up inside one of those quaint little tight-knit communities could feel unbearably repressive to a bright young child of God, longing to experience all the excitement and challenges of a world "out there."

No, the information revolution will not make us all the same. People could only believe that if they were to ignore all the evidence. Diversity is alive and well on the Internet, if not in our churches and shopping malls. And so is community. True community may be harder and harder to find in the old world, in our old definition of space and reality, but it is staging a comeback on the Web. As I said before, the human heart longs for a sense of community, and people will seek it out as long as they are still people. Many of us, and even more of our children, will be building new communities in the coming years. Those communities will take many forms and share a broad diversity of features, but one thing seems certain: they will be much less constrained by traditional notions of time and space than ever before.

SO WHERE ARE WE NOW?

We're still here, stuck in the same space-time continuum that our ancestors occupied. We may someday get to the place where we truly have annihilated time and space, where our immortal essence is imprinted onto computer memory and we live forever in whatever reality we choose for ourselves, or that is sinisterly chosen for us. Depending on your point of view, such speculations can be a lot of fun, really scary, blasphemous, a total waste of time, or all of the above.

We needn't consider such nightmarish or utopian scenarios to realize that the information revolution is changing conventional notions of time and space and, consequently, what constitutes and how we build and maintain community. But chances are, some of your most pleasant or deeply meaningful spiritual experiences still revolve around place and how you get there: visiting a shrine, viewing the sunset from a beach, trekking to a mountaintop. It's theoretically possible to simulate those experiences cybernetically, and someday we may, but in the meantime, "old fashioned" notions of time and space, or at least *place,* have their role.

And I think there's something about our old-fashioned notions of a community tied to place, a community you grow up in and that stays with you long after you've left it, that the human heart needs and longs for. However we construct our communities in the future, I don't think we'll find wholeness unless we figure out how to somehow capture that essence. How do we do that? We start by trying. I'm not even sure if technology can really help us in that regard; I only know it changes the landscape. And I can't help but be reminded of the Amish once again, who view technology with such suspicion, with such a keen evaluative eye, that I find it strangely respectful, as if they have a reverence for technology that we are lacking. Perhaps if we approached technology with the same sort of respect, we could figure out how to help it help us build the types of communities we really need and long for.

4

I Am My iPod

Christian doctrines are not answers to questions nobody asks,
but rather proposals for answers to questions everybody asks.
They are questions of ultimate concern and concerned
questions about what is ultimate.

—James Yerkes, 1999[1]

Human beings use tools; more than that, we fashion tools. We are a tool-using, tool-building life form. But as we have seen, the tools we fashion fashion us as well, and then we, refashioned, create new tools. In other words, we create technology, technology affects us, and we in turn create or, rather, refine, technology. Theologian and communications technology consultant Jennifer Cobb calls this "coevolutionary" process "a complex dance of becoming."[2] So who are we becoming? And how are emerging technologies changing who we are? These questions revolving around technology, change, and the unifying "lens" of identity are the focus of the next two chapters.

This chapter is specifically focused on *our* identity and how technology is changing the way we think about ourselves. The next will talk more about the identity of our machines and how we relate to them.

YOU SAY YOU WANT AN EVOLUTION?

I like using "evolution" rather than "change" to describe what happens to technology over time, and I'm not just trying to be dramatic. Change is just change; change happens all the time, and it's merely one small yet necessary step in the process of evolution. Evolution implies order emerging from chaos, and the world of information technology is pretty chaotic. Evolution also implies advancement or progress, though both terms are pretty value-laden and open to debate; a cynic might find "technological progress" an oxymoron, and who hasn't ever read a newspaper and wondered whether maybe God should have given the world to a "less advanced" species. But if we want things to get better, then first we have to believe that things *can* get better, which means we have to believe in the *possibility* of progress. Evolution allows us to believe that progress is possible in the midst of chaos and disorder.

The principle of evolution is that most changes drop by the wayside while others, by offering some sort competitive advantage, remain in the "gene pool" and get passed on to future generations, eventually changing the nature of the beast, as it were. It's a perfect analogy for how technology changes over time; technological changes—often introduced as improvements or enhancements but just as often introduced by accident or poor design—happen all the time, and most of them are somewhere between mild improvements that make little difference in the long run and completely useless, sometimes humorous, often disastrous, failures.[3]

A light reading of history might give you the impression that technological advances come about when brilliant inventors come up with radically new devices or ideas that change everything, but a more thorough understanding of how technology evolves exposes a much more chaotic process. Brilliant minds and radically new ideas have their role, to be sure, but so do accidents, tenacity, blind alleys, failures, and the caprice of public opinion and the economy. The orderly march of technological progress we often perceive is largely illusion and emerges from a relative chaos that for all the world looks to be governed more by random chance than by grand design. In other words, technological progress looks a lot like evolution.

But from a spiritual perspective, the real issue is how *we* change as the technology changes. I said at the outset that I would occasionally refer to my own religious beliefs, and this is one of those places where my beliefs are pretty central to the thesis I hope to develop in the next two chapters. I believe that creation is ongoing, that God isn't finished with us yet. I believe this both on a personal level—God isn't finished with *me* yet, therefore the fact that I'm not perfect doesn't give me a free pass—and on a corporate level—God isn't finished with *us* yet, so we, as a society and as a species can become more congruent with God's design. You could substitute desire, nature, will, intent, law, or probably any number of other words for "design" in that last sentence, depending upon how you have come to understand the nature of the Divine. I kind of like them all.

I believe God created humans in God's image, just as it says in Genesis, but that the use of the past tense "created" is God's perspective rather than ours. God, whom we may presume to be eternal and infinite, would necessarily have a different notion of time than we do, being finite and limited (see Ecclesiastes 3:14–15). God *is* (Exodus 3:14), but we are still *becoming*.[4] God is calling us to become fully human, to come into our God-image as true human beings. We might say that we are not (yet) really human *beings*—rather, we are human *becomings*. Okay, that's a little too cute, but you get the idea.

I accept that not everyone will have this view. Arguably it's a bit of a departure from traditional notions of the human condition and our need for atonement. Suffice it to say that if you believe, as I was once taught, that the human condition is static, that God is finished making us and that we have no role in that creation other than making a one-time choice for salvation, then what I say in this chapter may be of little spiritual consequence. If, on the other hand, you believe that the changes we undergo as individuals and as a species are in some sense related to God's intentions, then studying how technology evolves, and how we change in response, becomes a sacred endeavor.

TURN AND FACE THE STRAIN

Technology, particularly information technology, is closely associated with rapid, constant, seemingly relentless change. Societal forces pressure us to stay up to date by buying and figuring out how to use all the latest gadgets or services. Sometimes we relent and buy the latest, greatest thing, but then experience a vague sense of hopelessness when we realize it will be shamefully out of date by the time we get it out of the box. Meanwhile, pundits seem to delight in taunting us by repeating some form of the truism "change is the only constant." As a technologist, I am often an agent of change, so I have had a lot of opportunities to see how people react to it.

We have a love/hate relationship with change. Upon it we pin our hopes and dreams, and when we long for progress we complain that change happens too slowly. Yet we curse technological changes for the unnecessary grief they subject us to and the lack of real consequence they bring. "The more things change the more they stay the same" goes the old saying, and Qoheleth's refrain reminds us that, when it comes down to it, "there's nothing new under the sun" (Ecclesiastes 1:9 ff).

It's easy to be cynical about technological change, but that doesn't make it go away. Even if we don't try to keep up with it, it's still there, affecting those we love and the world around us. Change disorients us, and when we are disoriented we can forget who we are, lose our sense of identity. Perhaps this isn't all bad. One of the principles of transformational learning is that it's helpful, if not necessary, to be temporarily disoriented in order to think critically, to reexamine our hidden assumptions about the nature of ourselves and our reality so we can experience true growth, and be transformed into a better, more self-actuated person.[5]

I like to think of technology as part of what defines the landscape, the ground upon which we live and build the foundations of our lives and our spirituality. Change disrupts the landscape, makes the ground shake. Dramatic change can feel like an earthquake to us, and when we think we feel the ground start to rumble we're left wondering whether it's our imagination, a mild aftershock, or the beginning of the next "big one." We're all familiar with the notion of people finding faith when they're facing danger. I once heard a preacher talk about this phenomenon, how atheists will suddenly become believers when facing death, by saying that "when the ground moves [as in an earthquake], people look up."

If nothing else, all this technological change may get us to look up, to ask what sort of foundation our house is built on, and whether it is equipped to handle the next big one. I can't answer that question for anyone, of course. I can't even predict when the next big one is coming or what it will look like. But I can perhaps explain some of the tremors and point out a few places where the ground is shifting under our feet.

CH-CH-CHANGES[6]

Change was the watchword of the twentieth century. When I was a kid it was nuclear power, the H-bomb, the transistor, jet-powered aviation, and the space program that seemed to fuel all the angst and buzz about the accelerating nature of change in our time,[7] but lately it's been all about the computer and the Internet.

It will be interesting to see whether this perception of a constantly accelerating rate of change continues into the twenty-first century. The achievements of the space program were impressive and important in the abstract, but disappointing in light of where we thought we would be by now. Watch Kubrick's and Clark's *2001: A Space Odyssey,* the story of a manned mission to Jupiter, to remind yourself just how ambitious we felt in the days leading up to the Moon landing.[8] Better yet, see whether you can find a copy of the children's book *You Will Go to the Moon,* which explains the process by which the reader will take a vacation on the Moon when he or she grows up.[9] I really thought I'd be going. So did a few million other boomers. Do you suppose there's still hope? We're not getting any younger here! And whatever happened to that promise made by local power companies in one of those great little 16 mm films we used to get to watch in school that electrical energy would be so cheap they would do away with power meters? And why am I still grounded in this clunky old four-wheeled gas guzzler? Where's the personal supersonic plutonium-powered hovercraft I was sure to be piloting on the Moon if I managed to somehow survive into the twenty-first century?

Of course the future never turns out as people think, and I suppose it's human nature to overreach, to exaggerate the extent and potential of our achievements. I have little doubt that someday people will look back at all the optimistic talk generated during the so-called "tech boom" of the 1990s and wonder what the heck happened to all those great predictions. It doesn't mean all that talk was malicious or dishonest, or even that trying to predict the future is pointless and silly. If we are going to be conscious and open to the idea of evolution we need to entertain the possibilities of long-term change, even if we end up looking pretty foolish later on. And in spite of the disappointments, technology really has evolved dramatically since Kubrick released his classic film; the ground under our feet really has shifted.

But in the theory of evolution, most changes, in the form of "random" genetic mutations, are useless or even harmful. The same is true of technological change. How do we discern random, meaningless changes from true evolutionary forces? Can we develop a barometer for distinguishing evolutionary change, which really transforms our world and, ultimately, us, from changes that are meaningless or harmful? I don't know. I doubt it. It's a little like trying to predict the future: highly subjective and an imperfect science at best. We do the best we can, and we start by trying to become cognitive of the trends, rather than focusing on specific changes. Let me give a few examples.

Basic telephone service—or POTS (plain old telephone service) as it is affectionately known in the communications industry—is a good example of a technology with a lot of change and little or no real evolution. (Cell phones are another matter, but I'll postpone my rant on them to a later chapter.) Sure, there are all kinds of available "features" now, for a price, but the basic technology hasn't changed much from the system Bell used to call Watson more than a century ago.[10] The equipment may look a lot more modern than it did in years past, but am I the only one who believes phone service was a lot better in the 1970s than it is now, or that those old telephone bells—real bells—sounded a lot friendlier than all these chirps and obnoxious monophonic classic-rock ring tones? Perhaps, but I'll insist that there has been very little if any truly ground-shaking technological change in telephone service in my lifetime, let alone the last decade.

Now let's turn to the real culprit. Nowhere has the notion of constant change been more ingrained in the very nature of the technology than in PC hardware and software markets. People in the industry call this change "churn," and in many respects it drives the economy. If I build the best computer for the best price, eventually everyone who wants one will have one and I'll be out of business. But wait a minute, if I can build an even *better* computer next month, then some people who have my old one will want *that* one instead. I will be able to stay in business as long as I keep building "better" computers. It's the latest twist on the old planned-obsolescence theory (that you should intentionally design things to break or wear prematurely), and, thanks to Moore's Law, which says that computing power will double every eighteen months or so,[11] it keeps the whole technology sector pretty profitable and keeps all of us reaching for our Visa cards.

Of course, the real pressure for churn comes from the software side. Software developers are under intense pressure to bring their product to market yesterday, if not sooner, so naturally software comes out half-baked with tons of "bugs," small defects in the code.[12] We can hope that developers will eventually get around to exterminating the more obnoxious bugs, but most if not all of their energy has to go into developing new products; if they don't, their cash flow dries up and they're out of business in a heartbeat. So typically they'll concentrate their efforts on a new version of the software in which, if we're lucky, most of the bugs have either been fixed or are no longer relevant. The software company will then graciously allow you to "upgrade" to the new version by purchasing it at a reduced price.

So we are expected to keep upgrading to the latest version of the software we've come to love and trust (mainly because we've worked so long and hard figuring out how to use the cursed stuff). Eventually we get to a version that will no longer run on our old clunker of a PC, so we're forced to buy a new PC, and so the world churns. But what has really changed? Not much, in terms of true technological evolution. We're subjected to the stress of change, and encouraged to think of it as "progress," but the reality is that Qoheleth got it right. There's nothing new under the sun.

Besides churn, there's another way we're coerced into accepting pointless and unnecessary change, and it's prominent but by no means confined within the PC hardware and software markets. We call it "feature creep"—the strong tendency for technology marketers to add more and more "features" to products. They know that the more features they can brag about in their advertisements and on the outside of the box, the more likely we are to pick their product over those of their competitors, even though what we really want and need is probably a lot simpler, and hence easier to use and more reliable. My guess is that this is because we're so "value" driven; we don't really care how much we're paying for something as long as we get a "good deal." So if product B gives us twice as many features as product A but costs the same or only a little more, we would be fools not to go with B, wouldn't we? Sure, if we measure cost only in dollars. But what about the spiritual cost of all that unnecessary stress, all that pointless quivering in the mire beneath our feet? If product A does a better job of meeting our real needs and wants without mucking up our minds with a lot of useless features that serve mainly to confuse and intimidate us, wouldn't it be a better value, even if it were to cost *more* money?

The bottom line is that most changes in technology are like random genetic mutation; they're not so good. That said, PCs and other consumer technologies have evolved over time, and to some extent they have actually gotten better, or at least that's my story and I'm sticking to it. It's really up to you to judge, and that would be my bottom line advice: judge for yourself, but use some judgment. You probably have enough stress in your life without feeling pressured into unnecessary changes in how you use your computer, so ignore if you can, resist if you must, all the marketing pressure to constantly "upgrade," unless, of course, you really enjoy that sort of thing.[13] I must admit I do, so long as someone else is footing the bill. But with regard to change, the hoopla-to-benefit ratio is quite high in the consumer electronics world. There are some overall trends worth keeping an eye on (and I'll try to point out as many of these as I can), but an awful lot of what passes for revolutionary change in the industry is mostly just fanfare.

On the other hand, sometimes truly ground-shaking evo-lutionary changes start with little "mutations" that seem barely worth commentary. Who knew that an opposable thumb would lead to all this? If we must learn to ignore some of the more obnoxious changes in our technology, then we probably also need to learn to pay a little closer attention to some of the more subtle ones. Perhaps changes in how we encounter each other in the new "world" (formerly known as cyberspace) belong in that category. Let's close out this chapter by taking a closer look at one of those encounters, where issues of technology and identity come to light in an overt way.

WHO ARE YOU?

How do you present yourself to others when you are online? How do you imagine or conceive of yourself? And who are these other people, really? How do you know this person, this "friend," this companion is who she presents herself to be?

When we encounter others face-to-face, there are a multitude of rules and customs in play, most of which we are unaware of unless someone gets one of them wrong. Encountering people online is pretty much the same, but the rules and customs are quite naturally different and not as well established. Consequently, we are more likely to suffer transgressions, and thus be aware of the rules (or lack of them). And as with face-to-face encounters, the rules are not the same for everyone and every situation. That fact alone is sufficient reason for me not to attempt to give a primer here; you'll have to work these out for yourself. That's not to say you need be entirely on your own; there are any number of folks out there who will give you a tutorial in online etiquette, sometimes known as "netiquette,"[14] but such rules and conventions are best studied and practiced in the context of one, or at least one type, of community.

To the uninitiated, one of the most unsettling things about online community is how easily people can masquerade as someone they are not—changing their age, gender, or personality to suit their purposes. Let's be clear: The Internet is a dangerous place. You should be careful of strangers, especially if you're a child. There are people out there who will deceive you about their intentions, misrepresent themselves, or outright lie to you. But this should come as a surprise to no one. It is the world, after all, and why should the information highway be any different than our county roads and city streets in that regard?

Crime is nothing new, and deception was no doubt invented about the same time as sex. If you create a new social context, you are bound to encounter new methods of deception, especially if sex or money is at stake, and we all know there's plenty of both on the Internet. Typical venues on the Internet make identity deception pretty easy, since they rely solely on text for personal exchanges, but isn't that pretty obvious?

The truth is that we all hide to one extent or another in our encounters with each other. It's a defense mechanism; if we put our whole true selves out there to be trampled all the time, we wouldn't last very long. We all put up false fronts, masks that we can hide behind. I have found successful pastors to be particularly good at this sort of wall-building simply because they would be way too vulnerable without it. I talk to them and I can almost see them laying the bricks as they speak. Some of us, perhaps all of us, never completely come out from behind those walls, even around those closest to us, even to God, and hence we close off a part of our soul, never fully accepting our true nature.

But that doesn't mean we need bare our souls to everyone we meet. That would be obnoxious, if not deadly. And role-playing can be a lot of fun, even therapeutic. Encountering people online can give an atmosphere of ease and lightheartedness to the process. For me, the ethical boundary lies somewhere between hiding and role-playing. If I pretend to be someone else in an online seminary class, where folks are expected to encounter each other honestly and openly, that would be hiding, and consequently unethical, or at least unhelpful. The funny thing is, having observed a great number of classes meeting in physical space as well as in cyberspace, I would say there's a greater tendency toward openness and honesty in the latter.[15]

It's easy to hide in a "normal" classroom: just smile a lot and keep your mouth shut. In an online class, you can't keep your mouth shut (so to speak) because if you did no one would know you were there and you would fail the course. In keeping your mouth shut, you would also not get your money's worth from the course, for it's only when we try to articulate our deepest thoughts and emotions that we can begin to blaze new trails.

In an online environment, introverts come out of their shells, and extroverts sometimes have to shut up long enough to choose their words carefully.

On the other hand, there are places online, such as MMORPGs (massive multiplayer online role-playing games; often shortened to MMOs), where one is *expected* to pretend to be someone else. In these games people are encouraged to experiment with different identities and are able to try on a different persona or social role.

But what does all this online role-playing do to a person's psyche? How can you ever know who you really are if you're always pretending to be someone or something else?[16] I wish I had the answer. I imagine there are people who do go off the deep end in this regard and truly do lose themselves. On the other hand, the Internet might just be a safe place for people to test-drive an identity: to experiment with different personality traits, to try being more aggressive, passive, feminine, masculine, bashful, boastful, sarcastic, exuberant, perky, or cynical and along the way discover who they truly are. Through this playful experimentation we might just uncover attributes of our true selves that we would never know about otherwise. Isn't such experimentation what all kids do one way or another anyway, in the way they dress, talk, cut their hair, and so on? Perhaps part of the reason young people are so much more likely to spend a greater portion of their time online has less to do with their technical savvy than it does with their developmental needs.

Of course, I could be all wet. I don't think anyone really knows what all this online role-playing will do to us as a people, but it seems a pretty safe bet that it will change how we think about ourselves and, ultimately, who we are. I think it will eventually change our very concept of identity itself. According to media icon and former director of the Center for Technology and Culture (University of Toronto) Marshall

McLuhan, we really didn't even think of ourselves as individuals, as *selves* really, until the rise of print.[17] How much more will our sense of self change as we use this new medium in a new way, where everyone is a publisher and free, or at least freer, to try on different identities? Perhaps it amounts to nothing more than an expanded interlude of self-discovery, some might even call it computer-enhanced narcissism. But it has the potential at least to be one of those subtle chance "mutations" that works its way into the gene pool and takes us to the next step on the evolutionary ladder. I offer it only as an example of the type of thing we should be looking for, the type of subtle change in the way we think about and define ourselves in relation to each other. What I find so intriguing about online role-playing is that, somewhat contrary to the subheading above, the driving question at work in all this is not so much "Who am I?" but rather "Who am I becoming?" It speaks directly to the question of how we are living into God's image, how we are becoming the fully human beings of God's ongoing creation.

But this new media is still changing. It remains to be seen what will happen to text-based norms of interchange once market forces push us toward broadband communication. If voice and live video supplant "chat" and text, the nature of the medium will change dramatically, at least with regard to those features that McLuhan seems to be focused on, namely visual and aural versus abstract and printed. It will still be possible to hide and deceive in such an environment, but some of the innocent playful spirit of the medium might be lost. I suspect a lot of us will someday wax nostalgic for the "good old days" when people could reinvent themselves on a daily basis.

In any event, it seems the world of the future will increasingly exist for us online. Who we are online will just be who we are, period, in keeping with the suggestion made earlier that we just call it "the world" rather than "cyberspace." Online identity is already of more direct consequence socially than face-to-

face identity for many people, such as online teachers or learn-
ers or the growing number of people whose fame and fortune
come by way of their blog or their MySpace page. Who's to say
which personality, the one projected online or the one projected
face-to-face, is the real deal? Perhaps both. Perhaps neither.
Perhaps, someday, the question will seem terribly quaint.

5

ARIGATO, ROBOTO

It ain't all buttons and charts, little albatross. You know what the first rule of flying is? ... Love. You can learn all the math in the 'verse but you take a boat in the air that you don't love, she'll shake you off just as sure as the turn of the worlds. Love keeps her in the air when she ought to fall down, tells you she's hurting before she keels. Makes her a home.

—Malcolm Reynolds, a few centuries from now[1]

In the last chapter we dealt with the changing nature of technology and how technology relates to identity. In this chapter we'll continue with the theme of technology and identity, but shift the focus to *relationship*, examining how we relate to our technology, to our machines. While the previous chapter focused on our identity, this one will focus more on the identity of our machines, or, more accurately, how we *perceive* their identity. The question driving this chapter is how we can get along with our machines, how we can live in *right relationship* (a.k.a. *righteously*) with our creations.

The answer, stated simply, is love. But how can you bring love into a relationship with a machine? I might say I "love" my new universal remote control, meaning that I enjoy processing it, that I believe it to be extremely well designed and particularly useful, or that I'm glad I bought it. That might be a step in the right direction; it's certainly nice—one might even say spiritually comforting—to feel pleased by some object, presuming we're not starting down a road that leads to greed or idolatry. But it doesn't exactly feel like the type of love Jesus invoked in describing the two greatest commandments, admonishing us to love God and neighbor (Matthew 22:37–40; Mark 12:30–31; Luke 10:27), or the greatest of spiritual gifts Paul spoke so eloquently of to the Corinthians, telling them that love "bears all things, believes all things, hopes all things, endures all things" (1 Corinthians 13:7). And what about when we're not so pleased with our technology? Where does love fit in there? We'll put up with a lot from someone we love—sometimes that's how we know we love them—but we can't love a machine like we love a person, can we?

Perhaps not, but we do sometimes treat our machines like persons, and I think there are times we should; it helps us to get along with them, to have a good relationship with them. Clearly, machines are not people—indeed part of what it takes to get along with our machines is understanding how they are different. But that doesn't mean we shouldn't ever treat them like persons, or that we can't use the same principles for good relations with each other—principles like love, tolerance, understanding, and good will—as models for how to get along with our machines. Ultimately it helps us to get along with them better, to have good relationships with them so that they can better serve us.

I'm drawing a distinction between people—human beings—and persons, creatures with a personality. Admittedly it's an unconventional distinction, and it might make more sense to you after I have had a chance to offer a little more explanation near the end of the chapter, but first I want to address what may be the more troubling aspect of what I just implied, namely how we can think of our machines as lovable creatures.

KAYLEE, SERENITY, AND THE GIFT OF KNACKS

If you were really alert in the fall of 2002 you might have noticed a short-lived television series called *Firefly*.[2] It was a science fiction yarn, atypical of the genre in a number of ways, starting with there being no alien life forms, just humans, with all their usual foibles. The only other characters are their animals, livestock generally, and their technologies, which are at once futuristic and primitive. As the actors prance around in their rather nineteenth-century-looking garb brandishing Colt pistols and Winchester rifles (with the occasional laser cannon thrown in for fun), shoot pool in twentieth-century biker bars on holographic billiard tables, and fly around the "'verse" in rusty spaceships, your first impression might be that only Hollywood could come up with such a ridiculously unrealistic rendering of the future.

True enough, but the more you investigate this imaginary world, the more realistic the scenario starts to seem, particularly with regard to technology and the human condition. The world of *Firefly* is neither utopian nor dystopian. We seem to have overcome some of our plaguing problems—there's no apparent vestige of racism, for example—but most of them, like greed, cruelty, and bad government, are alive and well, and technology has created new opportunities for them to take their usual toll on human suffering.

Firefly's characters roam about a new solar system— we've apparently outgrown the old one—in an unimpressive bucket-o-bolts called *Serenity*. It's worth noting that no one ever calls the ship "the *Serenity*," she's just "*Serenity*." This tips us off to the fact that *Serenity* is one of the central characters in the story. This is a bit odd since *Serenity* has no overt personality, no "ship's computer" that gives her a voice or anything resembling cognizance; she's just a machine, vaguely reminiscent of a submarine in some old war movie. But that just makes it all the more fun to watch the series seeing "her" as a character, and studying the relationships between the ship and the crew members, especially Kaylee.

Kaylee is the ship's engineer, well, "mechanic" actually ("engineer" would be a little ostentatious for this setting and Kaylee is about as unlike *Star Trek*'s Scotty as *Serenity* is the *Enterprise*). Kaylee is young, pretty (in pseudo-plain Hollywood tradition), cheerful but not perky, enamored with girlish finery but usually seen with a little grease on her face, constitutionally incapable of violence, and has a relationship with *Serenity* that's nothing short of touching.

Kaylee obviously has a knack when it comes to machines. "Where'd you learn how to do that, miss?" Captain Mal asks when she performs some miracle of repair, inadvertently showing up the soon-to-be ex-mechanic of *Serenity*. "Just do it, that's all," she replies matter-of-factly, like she's never thought about it before. "My daddy says I got natural talent."[3]

Of course her gift is not all instinct; she does really know her stuff. In another episode we see her at a high-society party talking shop with a gaggle of admirers who are plainly impressed by more than just her good looks, and at various points in the series we see her speaking with authority about things technical, appearing not to realize that she's talking way over the heads of anyone listening. Such knowledge doesn't just come about through "natural talent"; she has obviously taken the time to educate herself and pay attention to how things work. Machines talk to her, and she knows how to listen.

At one point *Serenity*'s engines fail unexpectedly, causing a fire that consumes most of the ship's oxygen and knocking out life support. We see Kaylee in a rare moment of depression. She knows the crew is doomed. She's sorry for them, devastated by an overwhelming sense of personal failure, but it almost seems as if she's sad most of all for *Serenity*. "I'm sorry, Cap'n, I'm real sorry. Shoulda kept better care of her. Usually she lets me know when something's wrong. Maybe she did, I just wasn't payin' attention, or ..." The captain interrupts her, tries to bring her out of her funk so she can get on with repairs. He doesn't yet comprehend that even Kaylee has her limits, that what she does isn't anything like pulling a rabbit out of a hat, that getting machines to work isn't some voodoo slight of hand, that without a critical replacement part from off-ship she'll never run, and the crew will never breathe again. "Sometimes a thing's broke to where it can't be fixed," she tries to explain. Of course it's television, so we know it will all work out somehow, but to the scriptwriters' credit there are no miracle cures; no one pulls a MacGyver and makes a new part out of paper clips and duct tape.[4]

I identify with Kaylee as the person who's expected to make *Serenity* work; my relationship with technology consists mostly in trying to get the darn stuff to work, even if my job is more often focused on the people using the technology. I don't know how you would best describe Kaylee's relationship with *Serenity*, but I'm sure the word *love* is in there somewhere, and it's probably not going too far to say the rest of the crew loves *Serenity* too. But I don't think that quite says it right. It's more like the love that's inside them finds expression in the way they think about and interact with what is, after all, just a pile of hardware. For Kaylee, I believe that love finds expression through her "knack."

Perhaps you know someone like Kaylee. There are such people. They're not quite so Hollywood, but there are people who have a knack for making things work. In Hollywood such people tend to have either superior intellect or supernatural powers. I like Kaylee because, a little like the real deal, she has neither and both. She's charming and bright but she's not portrayed as some super genius, and there's no more role for magic in the imaginary futuristic world of *Firefly* than there is in ours. There is something a little magical about Kaylee's "natural talent," but nothing supernatural; she has simply followed her bliss and discovered her knack.

Chances are you have a knack for something, something that people tell you you are good at or that just seems to come easily for you. Often we don't know what our knack is because it seems so ordinary to us; we assume everyone has the same ability. Or maybe we don't even think of it as an ability. Maybe, like Kaylee, we "just do it, that's all." A knack is part science, part magic. Magic isn't quite the right word, though; magic implies some miraculous suspension of physical law. "Metaphysical" might be better. A knack lies in some small part beyond physics, but it doesn't defy physical law, just wholly satisfactory physical explanations.[5]

A knack is entirely acquired; no one is just born with one, though factors early in our lives—including what we are born with, which I can't help but believe is more than just our genes—are a big influence on what we ultimately acquire. That said, a knack goes beyond what is simply learned. Coming from one of the outer planets and being so young (she asks her parents' permission to work on *Serenity*), we can presume Kaylee didn't go to some fine engineering school and no doubt lacks a lot of the knowledge she would like to have, but she has acquired a good deal of skill, most important her ability to "listen" to *Serenity*—something she was neither born with nor would have necessarily learned in an academy. The best way to put it is that she has "nurtured her gift," and nurturing gifts is always a spiritual enterprise.

Hollywood tends to neglect the science side of a knack. People who have a way with technology are portrayed two-dimensionally, shallowly, and just have unexplained miraculous abilities to, well, perform miracles. Computer wizards do random trills on keyboards while high-resolution graphics dance across the screen at lightning speed, bringing up whatever knowledge or performing whatever task is required within milliseconds of someone deciding he wants it. The message: don't try this at home; leave it to the computer wizards.

I'll let you in on a little secret: real computers don't work like that, and there's no such thing as a computer wizard. Sure, we have all met some pretty freaky geniuses who have a knack for computers, the kind of people for whom it all seems so easy you wonder why you even bother trying, but there are no Harry Potters out there who can just wave their cyber wand at a computer and get it to perform whatever IT miracle the script calls for.

Getting along with computers and getting them to be your friend and give you what you want can be pretty hard work. The real trick is knowing what they can give and what the heck you really want; the rest is usually pretty straightforward. Those who are good with computers have gotten that way by being willing to do the work, probably because they love it. In short, they have taken the time to nurture their gift, to develop their knack.

In real life I think we tend to neglect the magic side of a knack. We get bogged down in all the technical knowledge we need to use our computers—and I won't for a minute pretend that we don't need it—but we forget that, ultimately, we have a relationship with computers, and that relationship is more than just which icons we click on. As Captain Reynolds reminds us, it ain't all buttons and charts.

I've always had a knack for getting things to work, but that knack suffers when I forget to *listen*; when I forget that there are two sides to a relationship and I go charging in, too ready to fix whatever the problem is instead of listening to what the device in question is trying to tell me. In other words, I am less likely to succeed at having my way with a piece of equipment when I put too much stock in my mechanical abilities, and that works both ways: I can be overconfident, but, especially with computers—simply because there is so much to know—I am more likely to be under-confident, thinking that I can only succeed by virtue of my knowledge and being all too aware that my knowledge is sadly deficient.

I make out a lot better with computers if I stop trying to be smart and start believing that I'm gifted. I can get a computer to do what it's supposed to by simply laying hands on it. Okay, I don't really believe that, but I love it when other people do. And it does happen. Someone's computer is acting up, she calls me for help, I come in, get my knack on, put my hands on the keyboard, maybe offer a silent and barely articulated prayer, and voilà, everything is fine.

Coincidence? Sure. Why not. I don't particularly care what actually happened, so long as the person who asked for help is happy. I can't explain it, and I can't rely on it. Most of the time I have to fix problems the hard way, logically figuring out what the heck is going wrong and what I have to do to correct it. But I do know this much for sure, even if I can't totally explain it: I get along with computers a lot better than most people do, and it has little to do with what I *know*. For lack of a better word, I tend to call it an "attitude," but it's really about relationship; it's really about love. And yes, you definitely *should* try this at home.

HOW ARE YOU FEELING, DAVE?

Serenity was just a machine with, as I said before, no overt personality, or at least not one we would consider very human. But let us consider a more traditional science fiction scenario. How do we relate to our technology when it starts to exhibit human behavior, like the HAL 9000 depicted in *2001: A Space Odyssey*?[6] Does a machine that displays humanlike intelligence become more lovable, or just more of a threat?

The mimicking of human intelligence has been the starting point for a lot of discussion and speculation about our relations with technology, often opening with or revolving around some version of the Turing Test, named after World War II hero and computer scientist Alan Turing. The test has various forms and permutations, but the basic idea is to test a computer's ability to fool humans into thinking it's human; or, stated the other way, test our ability to determine that a computer is a computer and not a human being. The question implicit in the Turing Test is "What happens next?" What happens when someone designs a computer that cannot be distinguished from a human being? What does that imply about the human condition, our relationship with machines, and our role as creators? If we've created something that can't be distinguished from a human being, doesn't that make us gods, or at least blasphemers?

Perhaps it will help if we construct an actual scenario. What if a team of computer scientists designed a program to interact with others online, pretending to be human. What would it take to fool people? Well, not a whole lot I suspect, but let's make the test a little harder; let's say we team the computer up with a dozen or so real humans, form an online community, inform the public at large that one of the community members is computer-generated, and challenge people to figure out which one it is. You begin to see the difficulty of setting up the test at this point; some people are bound to pick out the android, but how do you know whether they really figured it out or just guessed correctly? Perhaps the test would be more meaningful if we asked a team of psychologists to make the determination and ran a statistical analysis on their answers.

However we set up the test, the basic question is the same: Can a computer demonstrate sufficient intelligence to fool people into believing it is human? Actually the more we try to legitimize the test, the more I think we miss the real point, which can perhaps be best articulated by rephrasing the question slightly: Can a computer demonstrate sufficient intelligence to fool people into believing *she* is human? That is the real question for this chapter: Can a computer be a person? If you made friends with someone online, and later found out your friend was just a bunch of algorithms created by a team of computer scientists at MIT, how would you feel about it? Foolish? Betrayed? Confused? What would such an event signify?

When Turing proposed his test, computers were extremely primitive by today's standards. Sure, they could do some pretty impressive calculations, but few people ever believed they could do much more than that. The possibility that one of these banks of vacuum tubes, one of these power-guzzling monstrosities, one of these overgrown abacuses, could ever fool anyone into believing it was human for even a few seconds seemed pretty remote. It's a testament to Turing's vision that he could even conceive of the test that honors him.

The Turing Test is really all about intelligence, and it asks more about the nature of human intelligence than it does about the nature of computers. Can human intelligence be essentially reduced to a collection of algorithms? Is the human mind simply an amazingly compact, efficient, incredibly powerful computer, processing data organically in a way somehow analogous, however far removed in actuality, from the workings of an electronic computer?

These are deep questions, and the Turing Test merely raises them; it can't answer them definitively. My "answer," such as it is, is that human identity is a synergistic melding of mind, body, and spirit. Every day our machines threaten to surpass, and in many ways already have surpassed, us in terms of mind and body. Robots perform not-so-routine mechanical tasks at a skill level that far surpasses the abilities of the artisans who helped train them, and computers have defeated grand masters at chess, something it was once thought they could never do because they would forever lack human intuition and ingenuity. Surely it's only a matter of time before we'll be forced to concede that our machines are better and smarter than we are at nearly everything we used to say made us the paramount life form. But will we ever fill out the equation; will we ever create "artificial spirit"? Essentially that is the question *2001: A Space Odyssey* and countless other stories have asked us to struggle with, going back to *Frankenstein*[7] at least, and probably further, and when it comes to figuring out how to get along with our machines, the question has never been more relevant and more pressing. I don't know the answer, other than we should continue to struggle with the question, which means at least entertaining the possibility that the answer is "yes," that our machines, our creations, could someday have "spirit." In some respects I think they already do. Of course I think trees and rocks have spirit, so I may not be the first person you want to ask.

Originally, the question posed by the Turing Test was whether or not artificial intelligence was even possible. Now we take that as a given, so the questions have become more nuanced. Artificial life may seem the stuff of science fiction at this point, but we have already let the genie out of the bottle. Sure, you probably don't find your kid's Tamagotchi (a simple watch-size toy that needs to be "fed" and cared for) very threatening, or all that cuddly for that matter, but when advances in artificial intelligence meet up with advances in biotechnology, hang on to your cats, ladies and gentleman. Of course that presumes that life is essentially biological, and that may be mere human prejudice. I'm speculating, of course; we may never create "artificial life," and if and when we do I expect it will be much like artificial intelligence; we won't have solved all the riddles or erased all the distinctions, we'll have just blurred the lines and created new riddles; the questions will become more nuanced.

The rather rhetorical question suggested by the Turing Test is what difference does the "artificial" part of the term *artificial intelligence* make, if we literally can't tell the difference? When we start asking what difference the "artificial" part means when talking about life forms, the philosophical waters will become even murkier. I think an encounter with a superior life form is only a matter of time, perhaps within your lifetime, but I don't think it will be extraterrestrial; I think we will have created it; it will be an "artificial" life form. Of course we'll have created it with the assistance of a lot of artificial intelligence, a lot of computer assistance in other words, so if our creation of "artificial" life makes us somehow gods, our machines will be right there in the mix with us as co-creators.

But not everyone will be comfortable with this idea of humans, let alone machines, as co-creators. We are clearly creative beings. If we are created in God's image (Genesis 1:26), we can infer that we get this creative impulse in imitation of our creator, but have we gone too far? Will we ever see Shelley's nightmare become a reality? Will we ever create life, commit the ultimate blasphemy, supplant the role of God by building some monster that passes itself off as human?

We never will and we already have. We'll never truly create life in the way God did, but we have already created a great deal, including machines that think and toys that act cute. Frankenstein was as much or more a metaphor for the nineteenth-century human condition as it was speculative fiction. We were feeling the effects of the scientific age and coming to terms with our role as creative beings, plumbing the secrets of the universe. Should we deny that role? Can we doubt that God intended us to be this way, to be co-creators, as it were?

I say we should carry on creating, with care and love, but not put so much emphasis on human intelligence. Do we value human beings in proportion to their intelligence? If educators told you that one of your children was unusually gifted, would you love that one more than the others? The Turing Test is rigged. It's anthropocentric in the extreme, equating human behavior with value and respect. As long as we conceive of tests and milestones that measure how well our technology measures up *to us*, we'll create anxiety over how we measure up *to it*. Any standard that assures us of our superiority can only be temporary, and sooner or later we'll find ourselves in the unenviable—and ultimately fatal—predicament of the heroic railroad worker John Henry of the old folk song. John Henry was willing to die trying to prove that he was as good at busting through rock with his sledge hammer as the new steam-powered drill that threatened to take his job. We can empathize with John Henry and admire his spirit, his defense of humanity in the face of technology, but his effort was misguided. If we want to get along with our technological creations, we can start by not trying so hard to compete with them or allowing ourselves to be threatened by them. As their creators, perhaps we can learn to love them the way God loves us.

WHAT'S SMART TO A CAT?

This discussion started with the suggestion that it's possible, even desirable, to treat machines like persons. The fictional *Serenity* was one example, ostensibly a cold, rundown, somewhat temperamental machine that somehow manages to be a central character in an emotional human drama. Our discussion of artificial intelligence brings to mind another fictional character, Data, the android science officer aboard the *Enterprise* in *Star Trek: The Next Generation*. It's easy to see Data as a person because he is, after all, a human being, or rather he's played by one.

But do we value Data as a person because he's so smart or because he looks so human? No. We value Data as a person because he relates to us, and we relate to him. Data is perhaps a little too perfectly human in form and behavior to be considered seriously as a machine, but given the current state of the art, a real-world character essentially similar to Data is a lot closer than most of the technology we're asked to accept on *Star Trek*, and my guess is that most of us, if confronted with an actual Data-like artificial life form, would instinctively treat "him" (it?) like a person. Whether we would actually follow our instincts and treat him with the respect and mutuality due such an intelligent life form is an open question; a real-life Data would be pretty disturbing—until you got to know him.

But a machine he would still be. We would most likely act as if he were human, but he wouldn't be. There's a name for that delusion. It's called *anthropomorphizing*—treating or responding to nonhumans as if they were human beings, mentally reforming them into human beings so that we can instinctively relate to them. Cars lend themselves to this sort of anthropomorphizing better than most machines. Lots of people have names for their cars, and if you ask people whether their cars are male or female they may look at you incredulously or laugh at you, but they're just as likely to give you a straight answer. It's a little harder get so warm and fuzzy with a lawnmower or a bicycle, but who hasn't found themselves talking to a lawnmower that won't start or a bicycle with an untimely flat?

Anthropomorphizing is ubiquitous with regard to animals. People attribute human emotions, human motivations, even rational thought—something that humans themselves were probably incapable of early in their prehistory—to animals, especially our pets. And how can we avoid it? Our pets are not just *like* members of the family, in most cases they truly *are* members of the family; we share our homes, our wealth, and our love with them. Those who have lost one of these adopted members of the family know, and are perhaps surprised to learn, just how close they've become when measured by the extent of emotional devastation such a loss inflicts.

Pets are persons in that they have personalities. To some extent these personalities are projections of our own needs and emotions; but I don't see how people could believe animals don't have personalities in their own right if they have spent any time observing them, paying particular attention to the differences among individuals of the same species.

It's useful and appropriate to think of nonhuman animals as persons in this limited sense, but by definition they are not human, and the differences between us and them are usually pretty stark. Veterinarians and other animal behavior experts will be quick to point out that dogs and cats, with their smaller, less-evolved brains, have nowhere near the cognitive ability or reasoning power we routinely attribute to them. But then again, what's intelligence to a cat? And who's to say they are less evolved than we are? They've had at least as long to figure out how to be cats as we have had figuring out how to be humans, and cats are pretty darn good at being cats, much better than we could ever be, perhaps better than we are at being human. From a cat's perspective we probably look pretty dumb and less evolved.

But that's absurd. There's absolutely no reason to believe that a cat has any concept of "dumb" or "less evolved." A cat doesn't think of anything whatsoever *in the way we think of it*. Heck, a cat doesn't even think, at least not in the way we understand the word *think*.

The truth is there's no way I can even begin to talk about what might be going on inside the head of a cat without invoking human paradigms, and I can only relate to cats by projecting my human emotions and cognitive frameworks upon them. For example, I occasionally tell people I have a cat that thinks he is a dog. Rationally, I know this to be an impossibility;

rationally, I can deduce that my cat lacks cognitive categories like "dog" or "cat," or even self-awareness, but it helps me to comprehend and appreciate the quirks of his personality if I suspend my disbelief that he thinks he's a dog. This may be inappropriate, it may be unscientific, but it's the best I can do.

An expert on cat behavior and cat physiology would have a much better idea of what motivates my cats and why they do so many of the wacky things they do. They would probably have a better explanation for why one of my cats pants, drools, smells bad, follows me around the yard, and comes when he's called (but still refuses to fetch, in spite of noble efforts on my part) than that "he thinks he's a dog." Even so, they would still have no idea what it's like to be a cat, or what's truly going on inside their fuzzy little heads. You can never enter their world; you can only project your world onto theirs, just as you do with other humans. Try as hard as you like not to, you still ulti-mately have to anthropomorphize.

Our relationships with our pets are different than our rela-tionships with our technology, but maybe not as different as we think. Our pets are generally a lot cuter and cuddlier than our machines, but there's a fair chance we understand our machines and what makes them tick no better than we understand our pets. If you were the engineer who designed something, you might find it pretty silly to anthropomorphize it, but other people may need to in order to relate to it, to project the love they have inside themselves onto the relationship, to have a spiritually balanced existence with it. And even the engineer who designed it can appreciate the machine's personality, its quirks and wonts that, though clearly not human, allow her to relate to it, to "listen" to it the way a veterinarian might listen to a sick cat, or the way Kaylee listens to *Serenity*.

Relating to our machines can be a lot like relating to our pets. We try to understand them as best we can, we discern their personalities, and we anthropomorphize. We try not to feel threatened by them. We give them names, we talk to them, we wish them well, we consider them friends, or at least neighbors. We get our knack on; we pray for them. Ridiculous? Sure, but no more so than believing my cat thinks he's a dog, or that he loves me. Call me crazy, but my guess is that people who have a name for their bicycle get a lot fewer flats. As technology continues to take on a greater and more extensive role in our daily lives, it will become increasingly important to our spiritual well-being to be capable of getting along with it, living in right relationship with it, learning how to love it, not necessarily in the way a technology buff or a techtopian might love it, not necessarily in the way people marketing it want us to love it, but in the way that Jesus advised us to love our neighbors *and* our enemies.

6

I CAN'T DRIVE 55

*If we permitted fones people would be forever foning each
other with their most immediate and frivolous thoughts.
They would make appointments with each other at a certain
place and time, and they would demand the use of timepieces,
and of private sleds to carry them at whim about the City.
The streets would fill with explosive, noisy machines and other
noisome things, because once the technology beast was
uncaged, people would want squawking private radios and
private sense boxes and a host of other things.*

—Mallory Ringess, many millennia from now[1]

I have to confess that I'm a bit of a speed freak. I like to go fast
and I love things that can go fast: fast cars, fast computers, fast
boats, fast bicycles, you get the picture. But when I took a walk
on the Appalachian Trail, mindful of the curious and enigmatic
relationship between technology and spirituality, a funny thing
happened. The first time I got in a car after spending several

days on the trail, I was absolutely terrified by the sheer velocity of our travel. It took all the self-discipline I could muster not to ask the driver to please slow down. But when I peered at the speedometer I was shocked to see that we were only going fifty-five miles per hour, a speed I found intolerably lethargic back home.

As I began trying to evaluate the very sharp contrast between the spiritually rich world of a life on the trail, spending day after day moving no faster than three miles per hour, and the rather hectic world I left behind, a world I was reminded of when I came into town, I started thinking of the trail as the "three-mile-per-hour world" and the other as the "sixty-mile-per-hour world." As time went on it seemed more and more appropriate to characterize these two disparate experiences of the world in this way, by referring to the characteristic velocities of trail life versus "civilized" life.

Much later it occurred to me that I might examine the relationship between technology and spirituality by thinking in terms of velocity or speed. This chapter is part of the result of that examination. First we'll look at how technology is often focused on velocity or speed, how it promises to take us where we want to go faster, and we'll ask whether it really delivers on that promise and how it alters our goals in the process. Then we'll shift gears a bit and talk about "slowing down," such as in the old admonition to "take time to smell the roses." What is technology's role here? Does using technology always mean going faster? Is it possible that we could use technology in a way that allows us to slow down a bit, that gives us a chance to appreciate the beauty of creation, take time to enjoy the gifts that God has given us? As in every other chapter, our primary motivation here is to start to develop some criteria and an evaluative framework for being selective in our use of technology.

WHERE ARE WE GOING?

Many technologies are designed to address some aspect of velocity, promising to get you to where you want to go, either literally or figuratively, faster than you could previously. The obvious examples are in the transportation arena, and we already talked about that a bit in chapter 2, with the example of how the automobile transformed our experience of the world, and in chapter 3, with how technologies make our world smaller by effectively shrinking distances as measured in time, "annihilating time and space."

But many other technologies appeal to our desire for speed as well. Computer technology in particular is focused on speed; what makes one computer better than another is invariably stated in terms of speed or power, and computing power itself is always measured in terms of speed, such as how many operations or "flops" per second it can perform, a billion or so being pretty typical nowadays.

Nearly every other emerging technology makes some appeal to speed, trying to win our affection by claiming to offer us increased efficiency or productivity, allowing us to do more work in less time. We should be careful not to let productivity or efficiency become ends unto themselves, and hence an idolatry, but I don't see any real problem with these promises as long as they are actually fulfilled, though often they are not. If we can spend less time doing the mundane things that distract us from our true ambitions, so much the better, so long as our ambitions are in line with our spiritual values.

But what are our ambitions? Computers have essentially doubled in speed every eighteen months or so.[2] By that measure, today we should all be spending a tiny fraction ($1/_{64}$) of the time we spent using our computers nine years ago. Does that sound about right, or would you say that you are spending *more* time at your computer than you were a decade ago? I'm guessing the latter. Though good computing systems can bring about huge productivity gains, particularly in the service sector, most people who start using a computer to do something because they think it will save time end up pretty disappointed. The reason is relatively simple: computers have a way of rearranging our priorities and goals. We may start using a computer because we think we'll spend less time, say, organizing the family photographs, but pretty soon we may find that our goal has shifted from creating a lasting and useful digital archive of photographs to figuring out how to master Adobe Photoshop.

Don't get me wrong; that's not necessarily a bad thing. Learning how to master Photoshop is an accomplishment that may reap numerous and important rewards for you. You will no doubt better understand the art of photography and visual expression through its creative use and will certainly better understand the nature of digital images and how they can be manipulated. You will also gain valuable experience that will help you learn other computer programs more efficiently, so there is a real productivity gain here, just not the one you intended.

We should evaluate technology in terms of how it dominates our time but also in terms of how it affects our goals and ambitions. When we do this we are likely to find that our priorities have shifted. This may be a good thing. Life is what happens after you make other plans. Learning how to use an esoteric computer program may reap unexpected benefits for you. On the other hand, if you discover, upon reflection, that the time you used to spend getting to know and being with your loved ones is now spent cropping, airbrushing, and color-correcting their digital images, you may want to reevaluate your priorities a bit.

Personally, I don't resent the fact that I spend so much of my life parked in front of a computer. What bothers me is that so much of that time is spent waiting for something to happen.

And somehow a "faster" computer never seems to translate into less time spent in front of it. And I'm not just talking about when they are acting up; even when computers are working exactly like they're supposed to they make us wait on them. Computers may be orders of magnitude faster now than they were a few years ago, but software always seems to bloat in direct proportion to processor speed, so the time spent waiting for computers to boot up and respond to commands has stayed remarkably consistent over the years. The end result is that PCs are still absurdly, inexcusably, excruciatingly slow.

The real problem is not so much that computers make us wait too long, it's that they make us wait too often. If someone tells you something will take half a second, you would rightly expect it to happen right away; half a second isn't even a full heartbeat; we would have to concentrate to even be aware of its passing. But half a second when you have clicked on an icon with a mouse and are expecting an instantaneous result—like you would get if you manipulated something in physical space—seems like an eternity precisely because you *are* concentrating on it; you have nothing else to concentrate on. It's not so much that all those half seconds add up to an appreciable length of time—but believe me they do—it's that half a second is more than long enough to distract you, to cause you to stop concentrating on what you were doing and to interrupt the flow of your thought. Think about that. The computer, a tool that is supposed to help you think, is interfering with your thinking.

Computers are thinking tools. Of course, as we have observed, computers are much more than just tools, but they should be at least that: tools that help us think. As such they are sadly lacking precisely because they are *too slow*. There's a lot to be said for slowing down, and for the most part I would like my everyday experience of the world to be more like the three-mile-per-hour world of the trail than the sixty-mile-per-hour world I tried to leave behind, but speed is not the enemy; often speed is the very thing we need to free our minds, to let us live in a three-mile-per-hour world. We need computers that are more responsive and that better anticipate our needs. A computer that was truly faster in this respect would free us to think more clearly, to live more fully into our work, into the task at hand.

When an Amish craftsman takes chisel to wood in the three-mile-per-hour world, he expects the chisel to respond instantly to the signals he sends with his practiced hands, and the wood in turn to respond to the chisel. He knows more about his chisel than most of us would think it possible to know, and he's an expert at using and maintaining it; after all, he made it himself. But he's not thinking about his chisel much when he's crafting a piece of furniture, other than maybe pausing to touch up an edge every now and then, and he's certainly not thinking about response times or "signals." He's thinking about how much to take off here, a little smoothing there, enhancing this line a bit over here. The chisel is an extension of his hand, and therefore his mind. He's being a true craftsman, and as a craftsman he finds the time spent making something productive at various levels, including spiritually; he finds blessing in his "simple" (as if you or I could ever do it) work.

Would master furniture makers put up with a power saw that took five minutes to "boot up" before they could use it, or another two minutes before they could turn it off and set it down without risking amputation? Why should a high-tech tool used for thinking be any less responsive than a primitive hand tool used for crafting wood? The best high-tech tools should at least come close to fitting our minds the way a master craftsman's favorite chisel fits his or her hand. If we can develop that sort of relationship with our tools for thinking, we are better able to experience our time spent in front of a computer as craftsmanship of a different sort, crafting thoughts and expressions, and find blessing in *our* simple work.

So how can we make our thinking tools more like a craftsman's chisel? Most of us can't do much in the way of designing better, faster computers, but we can do our small part to put pressure on the manufacturers to build better systems for us by voting with our consumer dollars, spending what money we have on the best hardware and software we can find, and not rewarding people who make junk that wastes our time, interferes with our thinking, or, worse still, tries to do our thinking for us.

More important, we can take steps to "tweak" our computers to be faster and more responsive. I'm not talking about über-geeky stuff like over-clocking your CPU or going over to the dark side with all sorts of hardware upgrades, but rather changing some of the default settings in your software, customizing tool bars and pallets to fit your needs and make them more intuitive to you, turning off or, possibly, turning on and learning to use certain features that allow the software to work with *you* more quickly and smoothly. It's a matter of investing a little time with your tools, the way a craftsman might take extra time putting just the right edge on a cutting tool, or making a custom-fit handle from a carefully selected blank of wood. You need not become a computer expert, but if we want to work in a three-mile-per-hour world it behooves us to get to know our tools the way good craftsmen know theirs.

Thus, examining how we use our computers while being mindful of velocity has brought us back to the realization that we have a relationship with our machines. If we get to know them better, and teach them to know us better, by way of customizing some of the settings, then they are less likely to waste our time. The beautiful thing with PCs is that we don't have to worry about wasting theirs; they're more than happy to sit there waiting on us; they will dutifully stand by, awaiting our commands, for as long as it takes, and will never feel the least bit degraded by their subservience.

Sitting in front of a computer doing millions of mathematical operations every second and sending text messages across a universal network of fiber-optic cable at near light speed may seem a little incongruous with a three-mile-per-hour world. But time spent in front of a computer can be a time of intense contemplation, meditation, or fellowship with others, and that's perfectly consistent. By evaluating our tools in terms of velocity or speed, looking beyond the normal measures of "productivity" to how they perform *in relationship* to us, how they respond and work with us, freeing us to focus our attention on where we are going and how we are getting there, we gain productivity of another sort. I like to think of it as "spiritual productivity." That productivity is compromised if we are persistently expected to struggle with or wait on the computer rather than being quietly present with our thoughts or other people. When we find ourselves in front of a computer thinking or saying things like "hurry up" or "come on already," we have left the three-mile-per-hour world and gone back to the sixty, stuck in traffic.

SLOWING DOWN

Which would you rather do: walk steadily down a wilderness trail at three miles per hour, or accelerate to sixty miles per hour between stoplights and traffic backups? Putting the question this way, I'm guessing most people would claim to prefer the former. But do they really? Judging by the lack of traffic on America's hiking trails and the unavailability of sidewalks and other pedestrian thoroughfares in our towns and cities, most of us would rather have dental surgery than have to walk anywhere.

If you are blessed with legs that still work, I highly recommend you try walking. Walking is good for the body, good for the mind, and, more important, good for the soul. You could do your walking on a treadmill, I suppose (though personally I'd go for the dental surgery), but I especially like walking outdoors, away from traffic, with a destination in mind. It's how I pray.

Natural environs are nice, but one of my most memorable and deeply spiritual walks was around the perimeter of Manhattan Island in October of 2001, shortly after the World Trade Center disaster. I could have covered most of the same ground in a taxi, but it wouldn't have been the same. It wouldn't even have been close. Maybe it's because walking is slower, it gives you time to take in the vista a little more deeply, to see more closely the faces of the people walking past; it allows time for your imagination to speculate on what their world is like, where they are going, or what they had for breakfast; it gets you out of your own head for a bit, even while you are totally tuned in to all the muscles in your body, as they work together in ways that transcend what the finest software engineers and robotics experts can only try to imitate.

I've heard that someone asked Gandhi why he walked all the way to a far town, spending several days on the route, rather than taking the train. He told her that the train might get his body there in a few hours, but his soul would still be back where he started. I don't know whether the story is true, but I think it says something important and says it near perfectly, though I think it has to do with more than just speed. Gandhi was known as an avid walker, and film clips of Gandhi show him walking at a brisk and deliberate pace, with younger, longer-legged admirers obviously struggling to keep up. I don't think walking is good for the soul because it's necessarily slower than the alternatives; I think the real benefit is the calming meditation that seems to come through walking, particularly long-distance walking—though walking even short distances can be a gentle reminder of the spiritual state that longer walks have brought you.

But of course I bring this up not as an advocate of walking, but because I see walking as a metaphor for the three-mile-per-hour world, which fosters a healthy spirituality, and as a model for how we approach a relationship with technology. For one thing, walking does not preclude technology. In fact, long-distance walking necessitates, or at least encourages, it. Shoes are optional, of course, but I consider well-designed and constructed footwear pretty necessary on all but the most gentle terrain. A sturdy pack of some sort is essential on any extended walk, and though I could use one made from leather and wood (old technology), I prefer the latest in space-age materials—anything to save weight. For the same reason, I carry plastic rather than clay water bottles, though either would involve technology. On overnight hikes I'll likely carry a water purifier, LED flashlight, gas stove, butane lighter, maps and compass, titanium cook pot, maybe even a PDA (personal digital assistant) or a cell phone, and the list goes on.

But a lot of technology is designed to appeal to our desire for instant gratification. It promises to give us the easy path to spiritual satisfaction, but the most it ever gives us is the picture-postcard version. Sometimes you just have to take the slow way to give your soul a chance to arrive with you. I discovered this "Gandhi effect" a while back, and if you are reasonably healthy and can walk comfortably for an extended period, you can try to duplicate my experiment. Try walking some place that's hard to get to on foot but which you can also drive to. In my case it was Mount Washington in New Hampshire, which has both a toll road and a cog railway to the top, but also a number of approaches by trail. I'll caution you that any approach up Mount Washington by foot will be pretty challenging and notoriously risky in terms of weather, which can turn deadly in the blink of an eye at any time of year, but surely you could find a less arduous example of a trail that leads to a significant spot that is also accessible by automobile.

If you visit the top of Mount Washington by car, and manage to do it at a time when the weather is cooperating, you will be blessed with magnificent views of the surrounding countryside. Seeing this in person is infinitely more inspiring than seeing even the finest photographs of the same vistas. But if you then return to the base and hike up one of the trails you'll arrive at the top with a different, and much deeper, appreciation for the altitude and the surrounding terrain. Even if the weather isn't cooperating and, as is so often the case up there, you can't see a bloody thing and it's all you can do to stumble into the visitors' center out of the blinding wind and freezing rain and snow (in August), you'll find your arrival there inspiring. Most of the people you see at the top will have arrived by car, bus, or train. It has always struck me how clueless they look, as if they have no idea where they are, as if their souls were still down at the base of the mountain.

So once again we are reminded that easy isn't always better. The bus or the tram will get you to the top, but if God gave you legs, why not use them? Why not accept technology that lets you "walk," living in the moment, taking in the sights and sounds around you, body, mind, and soul, but reject, or at least be very suspicious of, technology that promises to take you where you want to go instantaneously, without effort or toil. Why settle for the postcard version of the spiritual life?

GETTING THERE IS ALL THE FUN

There's a famous theory in physics called the Heisenberg uncertainty principle that serves as a nice analogy for the inherent tension between our desire for speed and our spiritual need to live in the moment. I suspect nearly everyone has heard of the uncertainty principle, even if they have no idea what it's really all about or why it's so foundational to the field of quantum mechanics. It has such a cool name, and I guess people like the idea that a bunch of eggheads who seem to be (okay, are) so much smarter than the rest of us came up with a theory that states that there are things that even they will never know. It's such an intriguing proposition, that we know we will never know, and though it has broad ramifications, the uncertainty principle is quite simple at its foundation. Since velocity is a measure of how long it takes to get from point A to point B, you can only measure it as an average over the distance between those two points. We can make those two points very close together, but we can never know the precise velocity at any one point; we can only know *average* velocity over a distance between two *different* points. Stated another way, it's categorically impossible to simultaneously know an object's exact velocity and its exact location. Actually, it's the whole notion of exact location, or exact anything else for that matter, that's in question here, but I digress once again into the dark side.

Recalling the uncertainty principle, it occurs to me that we can't know where we are if we know how fast we are going. In other words, if we're conscious of how long it's taking us to reach our goal, we can't be truly in the present. Living in the moment seems to be an important part of any spiritual discipline. I thought of this often when in the three-mile-per-hour world of the Appalachian Trail. I always found myself too focused on speed and distance; too focused on my goals for the day, week, and summer; too distracted by mundane matters of velocity to truly appreciate the infinite cascade of precious moments God was giving me.

It occurs to me that that may be what's wrong with much of our technology, why we intuitively seem to find it antithetical to a spiritual way of live. If our technology is totally focused on speed, getting things done more quickly or efficiently, then we're discouraged from living in the moment. It brings to mind that wonderfully ambiguous saying: "getting there is half the fun." That's my problem: I'm always thinking about getting there. Shouldn't the expression be *"being here is half the fun"*? Of course, it's still apparently only *half* the fun, and I don't mean to dismiss the importance of goals. Walks with a destination in mind seem more like pilgrimages and somehow always manage to feel more spiritual to me than walks that are just for the sake of walking.

If nothing else, examination of technologies through the "lens" of velocity should help us be more aware of this tendency, this desire to avoid living intentionally in the moment by distracting ourselves with toys that whisk us out of the environment at mind-numbing speed, leaving our souls far behind. Yet, ironically, sometimes our tools aren't fast enough, or, to be more precise, sometimes they're not responsive enough to our intentions, whisking us out of the moment by drawing attention to themselves when they should be merely mediating the experience. Either way, velocity is an important consideration in our evaluative process, as we seek out tools and technologies that, like a craftsman's beloved chisel, help us to live totally and fully in the moment, finding simple blessing in our daily toil.

7

NEUTRONS, NETWORKS, AND NEW MODELS OF GOD

If you want to learn about nature, to appreciate nature, it is necessary to understand the language that she speaks in. She offers her information only in one form; we are not so unhumble as to demand that she change before we pay any attention.

—Richard Feynman, 1964[1]

Like the previous chapters, this one looks at technology through a specific "lens." In this case, through the concept, or category if you prefer, of *connection*. When we think about connection, connections, and connectedness and examine technology from that perspective, ideas pop into focus that we might not have considered as deeply otherwise, even if we had been aware of them. This chapter is structured according to three such ideas, notions about technology that seem particularly salient when we think in terms of connection and connectedness.

The first idea is very general, so general that it is really more about science and philosophy than about technology, but it provides a foundation for how we might encounter technology with a new attitude. The second idea is quite specific in that it primarily focuses on portable telephones, "cell phones" in the vernacular, but it represents a broader, more general caution about the darker side of "staying in touch." The third idea deals directly with the idea of connection itself and how connections can form an entity unto it's own, a network. You find networks nearly everywhere once you think to look for them, but networks are unlike most "things" in the created world in many important and philosophically foundational ways. Networks are not really a new phenomenon, but with the rise of computer technology and the Internet we are becoming increasingly aware of them, and our way of thinking about and analyzing them is evolving into a new science. As we blaze new conceptual trails struggling to understand the behavior of networks, we may well find new ways of thinking about the Divine, new "models of God," to borrow a phrase.[2]

EVERYTHING IS CONNECTED

Has anyone ever told you that everything is connected? It's a cliché, but I can't help but think that it's still a profound truth. When I have struggled to find words to describe the indescribable moments in my life that I'm inclined to call deeply religious or spiritual, I inevitably resort to using traditional religious language, perhaps speaking of "being touched by the Divine" or even "catching a glimpse of the face of God." Those are attempts to invoke metaphors for an experience that transcends anything in my routine experience or normal understanding of the world. In such situations, the value of a religious tradition comes into focus; it gives us a language to talk about and reflect upon experiences that, though deeply personal, are not unique. The Bible speaks of "sighs too deep for words" (Romans 8:26, NRSV). Often I can only speak of an overwhelming "feeling of connectedness."

Connection seems to be a common feature of deep spiritual experience across religious traditions; if you ask people to describe their most profound religious or spiritual experiences, this notion of connection or connectedness will come up often. Perhaps you've even had this "feeling of connectedness" from time to time. The feeling—though the word "feeling" doesn't quite do it justice—is both abstract and personal; it's an awareness that not only all things, but all beings, including you, are connected in some terribly beautiful web of life and love. But beyond an awareness of connected*ness*, there's also an apparent awareness of the actual nature of the connections themselves, as though for an infinitesimal moment you actually comprehend the very nature of the universal web, as if we are normally protected from this awareness because surely our minds would explode if we experienced this awareness for any finite length of time.

So naturally I find it interesting to observe that some scientists are starting to focus upon the idea of connections or relationships as the true constituents of the universe, that the little bits of matter that make up the world are less real than the connections between them. Think about that for a moment. That's the exact opposite of the commonsense perspective. We're inclined to think only of the little bits of matter as real; the connections, the relationships between the bits, are only a mental abstraction—they have no *substance*.

That's because most of us have been raised to understand the world from a materialist perspective. The world, as we might well intuit and have certainly been taught, consists of empty space and matter, or "stuff." There's all kinds of stuff in the world: really, really big stuff; really, really small stuff; and everything in between. Sometimes globs of stuff bump into each other in various ways, producing diverse results, such as chemical reactions like fire (perhaps our first technology), and often creating new stuff out of old stuff, such as when the planets coalesced out of star stuff or when Adam was formed from the dust of the earth (Genesis 2:7).

If we look at some stuff, any stuff big enough to look at, sooner or later we'll figure out that it's made out of other stuff, and that stuff is made out of yet other stuff, and so on. Long ago scientists theorized that if we kept dividing these small bits of stuff into even smaller bits of stuff, eventually we would get to a bit that was so small it couldn't be divided any more, no matter how sharp our knife. They called this smallest possible bit of stuff an "atom." The atom was conceived, long before its existence was established empirically, as the fundamental building block of the universe. If we could discover it and solve its mysteries we would unveil the fundamental secrets of existence.

Of course, scientists refined their notion of the atom. We learned in our grade school science class that the atom is composed of even smaller bits of stuff we call protons, neutrons, and electrons, with their various combinations forming the basis for the whole branch of science we now know as chemistry. That in itself is not very disturbing; it just means the fundamental building blocks of the universe are a little smaller than the atom.

But in the middle of the last century, scientists actually started breaking atoms apart for the first time. A funny thing happened, and I'm not talking about the release of energy Einstein predicted and Hiroshima and Nagasaki experienced. It turns out there are all kinds of other strange (and I mean really strange) particles inside the atoms, or so it would seem. It started to look like the supposedly irreducible protons and neutrons are actually made up of many even tinier particles. This is starting to look familiar. Will we just keep coming up with sharper and sharper knives, so to speak, and keep finding smaller and smaller bits of stuff inside of the stuff we used to think of as the irreducible building blocks that our ancestors conceived?

No, because it's not so much that some subatomic particles are made up of other subatomic particles, but rather that these various particles—and scientists just keep discovering more and more of them as time goes on—essentially come into and go out of existence as we start messing with or even just "looking" at them. Of course these particles are too small to actually see in the conventional sense; we might even say they lack any quality we would normally associate with "substance." And you can't really see something that has no substance. The moon is tethered to the earth by gravity, but we can't see the tether; it's an abstraction we use to visualize the relationship, which can only be stated mathematically, and you can't see a relationship, you can only know it is there. Does that make it less real? On the contrary, I would say it makes it more real. It's our notion of "substance" that is the true abstraction.

Our stubborn insistence on thinking of the "parts" of the atom as parts in the first place makes it harder to conceptualize what goes on inside of them, and harder to understand this entire field of science called, ironically, "particle physics." Most of us can't help but think of these "particles" as little balls, little bits of stuff, but they're really not much like that. They're more like "clouds of probability," though, of course, even that's a metaphor for what's really going on and what even the most brilliant physicists can have trouble getting their minds around; they need to use the language of some pretty advanced mathematics to talk with each other. If you don't understand the math, you can't really understand what goes on inside an atom and, by implication, what the world is made of. What it boils down to is that the universe isn't made out of blocks after all.[3] I find that comforting. The idea of a "fundamental building block of the universe" strikes me as a rather childish notion, as if we could extrapolate from the image of a toddler playing with blocks the image of an all-knowing, all-powerful god in the act of Creation.

So what has all this to do with technology and spirituality? Everything. For starters, the whole divide between technology and spirituality, which is really a subset of the physical/metaphysical divide going back to the ancient Greeks, is based on a materialist view of the world where science, technology, and the "practical" arts deal with the material world, while religion, spirituality, and aesthetics deal with the immaterial or spiritual world. But if the world is actually composed of relationships rather than stuff, if the connections between subatomic bits are what are truly real, while the bits themselves are mere abstractions, the whole basis for the material/immaterial divide starts to fade.

Of course, everything we thought we knew about chemistry doesn't get tossed out the window just because we have discovered that electrons are not like little moons orbiting a subatomic sun, hard as it is to get that bogus image—an image that never was very useful and that no respectable physicist born in the last hundred years ever took seriously—out of our heads. And it's not as if spirituality suddenly becomes a science. But if we understand that the universe is not "made up" of sub-components, like blocks stacked by a child or even a god but, rather, that it is more a complex web of relationships and connections that can only be described in the musical, poetic, and, dare I say, magical language of mathematics, then science and technology start to look a lot more inspired and art and spirituality start to appear a lot more "practical."

For my part, I continually struggle to escape the constraints of a materialist worldview, the notion that the world is made up of stuff and that everything else is somehow less real, less "scientific," and in some cases, more sacred. As an alternative, I try to assume a "connectionist" worldview, where the true nature of creation is contained in the connections, relationships, and processes we observe all around us. It is in these connections that reality lies, where the real world is becoming in an ongoing act of creation.

It is also where the sacred resides. God, in the connectionist worldview, is not "spiritual" in the sense of other-than-material, but rather resides in and defines the essence of those connections, relationships, and processes. It also helps us find the sacred in the profane. When I observe the sun setting over a mountaintop, I think about the movement of celestial bodies and the relentless drift of the continents and am reminded of God. Who wouldn't be? But I also see God when I type at this keyboard and think of all the processes going on inside my computer as words pop onto a liquid crystal display—words full of meaning, words provided over the years by people in relationship with each other and to a culture, words that have additional meaning determined and refined by their relationship and proximity to each other. The simplest, most common, most profane things are loaded with connections, and are therefore holy.

If technology is no more connection-rich than anything else, it is certainly no less so. Connections and processes are certainly the very essence of computer technology, where the whole purpose is to run a series of processes we call a program and to respond to the various and sequential relationships between the millions or billions of bit states—which, with elegant simplicity, can only be either on or off—within its circuits.

Computers are quite probably the best example of how something incredibly complex and dynamic can come out of something incredibly simple and profane. After all, in the materialist/reductionist worldview, where physical reality is composed of complex arrangements of stuff, like so many blocks in some cosmic Lego set, the most powerful supercomputer is nothing more than a big bucket of bits, a bunch of ones and zeros stored on magnetic media and flying around at near light speed along metallic paths. A connectionist worldview, on the other hand, lets us see the computer in its true light, as an intricate, extraordinary, and profound piece of technology. In a materialist worldview, we can deduce that God might inhabit the circuits of a computer; to say that God could not would put a restriction on the movement or ability of God that most theologians would find unacceptable on principle. But a connectionist worldview allows us to imagine how God indeed *does* inhabit the circuits of a computer, as easily and as certainly as God is present in a sunset viewed from a mountaintop.

CAN YOU HEAR ME NOW?

As human beings, we have a fundamental desire, a primal need, to feel connected to the world around us, to each other, and to God.[4] Many technologies, particularly the ones we associate with the information revolution, can be seen as a way of extending our ability to establish and maintain these connections.

Yet more connectedness is not necessarily better than less connectedness. My 2002 hike of the Appalachian Trail (AT) changed my life in many ways and taught me many important lessons. Most of them are hard to articulate, let alone impart to others, but one at least is fairly easily described, perhaps because I learned it as much from listening carefully to other hikers' experiences as I did from observing my own: *beware of technology that offers to make easy connections.*

Simply put, there is something to be said for "getting away from it all," and technology has a way of making that nearly impossible. Carrying a small, lightweight radio into the wilderness is tempting, given that boredom is the real enemy out there, though few people get around to talking about it when they come back, given all the more interesting stories they can tell. And arguably, carrying a radio is an essential safety precaution, given the possibility of weather-related, natural, or even unnatural disasters. But doing so, even if you leave it off most of the time, maintains a connection to "civilization" that compromises one of the major attractions of the wilderness experience, an experience that I and many others find deeply spiritual. The presence of a radio in the wilderness is one of the few cases where I see something akin to a direct inverse relationship between technology and spirituality, where more technology means less spirituality.[5] I never carry a radio while hiking. I'll take my chances with the weather and al-Qaeda.

The piece of equipment I was most ambivalent about on my Appalachian Trail hike was a cell phone. Like a radio—actually, it is a very user-friendly, two-way radio, not unlike the walkie-talkies you probably played with as a child—a cell phone can be a critical piece of safety equipment, and in areas where there is adequate coverage it is arguably foolish to go hiking without one; it could well save your or someone else's life. During the portion of my hike when I carried a cell phone, I thought of it mainly as a lifeline to my family. I couldn't leave the phone on for very long because of battery issues,[6] but by using the cell phone to check in with them periodically they, in effect, had a way of reaching me; if there was some kind of family emergency that required my attention, they merely needed to wait until my next check-in. But naturally, these routine check-ins radically altered the quality of the wilderness experience. The profound loneliness of being separated from loved ones was, I believe, one of the most important determinants in making the trail experience a spiritual event. Left out there in the "wilderness," forced to confront life on life's terms in my own skin with only the occasional camaraderie of other hikers, strangers with a common purpose, is part of what makes a hike a pilgrimage.

Hiking the AT is not some harrowing survival experience, but long-distance, backcountry trail hiking is a milieu where you are encouraged to rely on your own spiritual resources and your relationship with a higher power. You are not so much confronted with matters of ultimate concern as you are liberated from the distraction of mundane crises, and emotionally vulnerable enough to have a radical encounter with whatever truths you discover. Routine telephone conversations with family are a blessing, to be sure, but they critically compromise that spiritually fertile environment. Calling my family was a great comfort, and in the final analysis probably worth the spiritual cost, but there was a cost.

Of course, once I had the cell phone I found it indispensable for other things as well. What I found most comforting, aside from calls home, was the ability to call ahead to a motel near a road crossing so I could assure myself of a room for the night before making the long walk or hitchhike into town. It doesn't take a lot of imagination to realize how phoning ahead for reservations might detract from the sense of a true wilderness experience.

A spiritual life, like the life of the Appalachian Trail thru-hiker, is a life of discipline and routine. I don't mean you have to do the same things every day; variety is good for the soul and essential to growth—spiritually, emotionally, intellectually, and physically—but there is something to be said for a simple routine, simple goals, and a simple one-day-at-a-time approach to life. Often we try to balance our otherwise hectic lives with extended periods of "down time," when we "get away from it all." It's not a bad impulse. Retreats and vacations may be important ingredients for a healthy spiritual life and may be necessary convalescences for wounds inflicted by life in the twenty-first century, but they're not enough. We are too willing to believe that we can "balance" our lives by partaking in opposite extremes. It's like believing a healthy diet consists of bingeing and starving, or that we are good stewards of the earth if we fence off a few acres of parkland, or that we are good parents if we spend a few hours of "quality time" with our kids.

If you look around to those who seem to be living spiritually mature and fulfilling lives, you don't normally find people who work really intensely at their spiritual life in workshops or retreats once or twice a year and then go back to leading hectic, out-of-control lives. It's the things we build into our "normal" daily lives that feed and nourish us spiritually: daily prayer, dedicated quiet time in the morning or before bed, the sanctity of the family dinner table, humble expressions of gratitude before breaking bread or partaking of life's other little joys. These "habits of the heart" are the things that really make a difference over time. And this is what concerns me about our increased reliance on technologies that make for easy connections.

When I see people yakking endlessly on cell phones, mostly I'm just annoyed. But sometimes I think back to my experience on the trail when I didn't have a cell phone and I feel a little sorry for these people. How long could they go without calling others and giving them an update on their lives? Perhaps they'll never find out. Sometimes I feel like I'm watching everyone around me shoot up heroin, unaware of their own addiction, and having no idea what they are missing out on or how empty their lives are becoming as they fill every waking minute with minutiae.

Of course, there is justification for a lot of this chatter. It's often part of our job or our social obligation to "stay in touch" or "network" with colleagues or clients. And that's the part I find so frightening. More and more, there is an expectation that we stay constantly connected. I have had people become indignant or suspicious when I've turned off my cell phone. (I've since gotten rid of it entirely.) Others have gotten angry or worried when I haven't responded to e-mail quickly enough to suit them, and it has become increasingly acceptable for employers to expect employees to be reachable "24/7." Thanks to the information revolution, we are living in a hyperconnected age, and I'm convinced the effect is toxic to our spiritual well-being.

Meaningful connections with loved ones and with our higher power are important and good. It serves us well if we can develop and deepen these connections, engage them routinely and often. But shouldn't we also be looking for ways we can "disconnect" from the minutiae of the world, resisting our inclination to lean on others in an effort to distract us from the routine joys and sorrows of life alone in our own skin?

"Self-reliance" is a sin in some religious traditions, the implication being that you shouldn't try to get through life on your own resources, but should rely instead on God. But that doesn't mean you shouldn't ever have to face life's little challenges alone. Going into the desert, into the wilderness, being "alone" with God, is one of the oldest and most central parts of all religious and spiritual traditions; it is an essential part of the religious life. Though the desert/wilderness experience archetype is generally a one-time, life-transforming event, most religious traditions find some way of bringing a piece of this critical experience into routine religious life. The practice of fasting during Lent is one example. Another is the practice, common among Catholics, especially those with a religious vocation, of taking a silent retreat, refusing to speak or communicate with others for an extended period of time.

So what should we do about all this hyperconnection? Here's my bottom-line advice: spend some time in the wilderness; go there often; avoid, to the extent possible, any technology that won't allow you to be there. How that translates into your own life is for you to decide. You could take me literally, strap on a pack, and head off into the mountains or woods, or you could take it as a metaphor. Either one, or both, is fine. My real concern is that as you evaluate technologies, deciding what impact they might have on your spiritual life, you consider how the connections they enable can be a two-edged sword; they can be life-giving, but they can also place restrictions on our ability to be alone with God.

IT'S A SMALL WORLD AFTER ALL

What does God look like in a connectionist worldview? That's a question that many theologians have addressed in one way or another, particularly those who struggle with the relationship between science and religion. It would be outside the scope of this book to try to capture their arguments here, but I will stress the importance of asking the question.

While some people are content to have one worldview for science and another for spirituality, I find such a condition untenable and ultimately unsatisfying. As a people of faith and integrity, when we can no longer believe in a god that is smaller than our experience of the world, we need to imagine God in ways that are at least as large as our understanding of the real. At such times, we must seek out new models of God, new ways of thinking about the Divine that challenge and stretch our comprehension. If our science leads us to an understanding of the world where reality is defined by connections and relationships, then a god defined by a materialist worldview feels incomplete at best. Sure, there are times when thinking of God as "the old man with the beard" is comforting, perhaps even the only way we can come to terms with the Divine, but there are other times when that model just doesn't cut it, especially as our understanding of society and the world around us deepens.

I believe networks have the potential to provide such new models. Not that they are *the* way to think about God, or that the old models are inferior or no longer applicable, but just that they can augment and enrich our understanding. It will be easier for me to explain my confidence in that assertion if I first explain a bit more about networks. As I do, I hope you will start to connect (no pun intended) some of the dots for yourself; to begin to appreciate how you might imagine the God of your understanding as a network, as a divine presence that lives in and defines the connections, that makes Love, Truth, Beauty, and Life (other names for God) the true constituents of the universe, the reality in which we live.

In the previous section, I likened a cell phone to a walkie-talkie. It's quite possible you've never made that association before. There are some technical differences in how the two devices operate, of course, but the essential difference between the two has nothing to do with the devices themselves. Both are, in essence, two-way radios, capable of sending and receiving voice messages wirelessly. The essential difference between them, what makes a cell phone a radically different technology than a walkie-talkie in terms of its impact on our lives, is alluded to by the fact that walkie-talkies usually are sold in pairs, while cell phones typically come with "a plan."

A single walkie-talkie is of no value to you if there isn't someone out there, preferably someone you actually want to talk to, with another walkie-talkie sufficiently like yours. What makes a cell phone so valuable is that not only are there countless other people with cell phones sufficiently like yours, but also that there is a whole *network* of telephones out there, a network in which your phone is but one "node." You can use your cell phone to talk to anyone else, anywhere in the world, who has virtually any kind of telephone; every "phone" everywhere on the planet is part of the same vast network. If we want to get technical, it's actually a network of networks, not unlike the Internet, but the difference is hardly more than semantic from the telephone users' perspective; at most, it means you'll have to punch a few extra numbers to get through to your "party."

Networks are a central feature of the information revolution and part of what makes it so revolutionary. The Internet itself is a network, of course, and it is the Internet (as much or perhaps more than the personal computer) that is transforming life in the twenty-first century. Indeed, it has long been predicted that an "Internet appliance" of sorts will replace the PC as the central consumer technology, though it seems the versatility and adaptability of the ever-evolving PC might assure it a role well into the foreseeable future.[7] Of course, the Internet is really just an outgrowth of the telephone network, which, though it continues to grow in both size and sophistication, has been with us for more than a century.

Networks allow communities to exist, as we have seen with the examples of the Internet and the much more established telephone network, but they also allow economies of scale by enabling multiple computers to work on a single problem. A classic example is SETI@home, where some of the unused capacity of your PC is amalgamated with hundreds of thousands of other PCs to form a virtual supercomputer, analyzing the data from radio telescopes in the search for signs of extraterrestrial life.[8] It's this notion of "distributed intelligence," where computing power is distributed over a network rather than centralized in a HAL 9000–like central megacomputer, the "mainframe" of yesteryear, that characterizes the modern approach to computing. Indeed, supercomputers are typically and essentially networked banks of smaller computers working together synectically.

But the "power of the network" is not just an algebraic, or even a synergistic, summation of its component parts. Indeed, its "parts" are merely connections and nodes, which apart from the whole are relatively powerless, if not meaningless. A network is an entity in and of itself, but it is an entity that is "composed" of connections and governed by rules of behavior that have little to do with the "stuff" of the network and everything to do with how connections are established and defined. As such, a network is an intriguing example of how a connectionist worldview can help us to understand reality. If we look at networks as the sum of their parts, as merely a collection of nodes, their behavior seems mysterious, even arbitrary. But when we stop thinking in terms of what is "on" the network and examine instead the connections that truly define networks, we can start to make valid predictions as to how they will behave.

The study of networks has become a new science. It started, by at least one accounting of its history, when people began examining the small-world phenomenon, made famous by the popular Kevin Bacon game on the Internet.[9] The idea of the Kevin Bacon game is to minimize the number of "degrees of separation" between Kevin Bacon and any other actor, living or dead. For example, if Charlie Chaplin appeared in a movie with someone who appeared in another movie with someone else who appeared in yet another movie with Kevin Bacon, there would be three degrees of separation between Charlie Chaplin and Kevin Bacon. If you can think of someone who appeared in a movie with Charlie Chaplin who also appeared in a movie with Kevin Bacon, you will have reduced Chaplin's "Bacon number" from three to two.

Ostensibly, the thesis that forms the basis for the game is that Kevin Bacon is at the center of the Hollywood universe. But this is a bit tongue in cheek. The real idea behind the Kevin Bacon game is that, when examined from this "degrees of separation" perspective, the world is remarkably small. In fact, it has been widely speculated (and I believe disproved, though only with great difficulty) that every person in the universe is separated from every other person in the universe by no more than six degrees, that, at most, you know somebody who knows somebody who knows somebody who knows somebody who knows somebody who knows, well, anybody. In truth, there are probably far fewer degrees of separation than six between you and anyone who is famous enough for you to know of his or her existence, probably only two or three, hard as that may be to believe.

Of course, the small-world phenomenon was only the starting point for what is proving to be a fascinating and paradigm-shifting area of research into the nature of networks and the connections that define them. What captured my attention, and what has me convinced that the science of networks is so wrought with potential, is that it has come about through collaboration across disciplines, with physicists, sociologists, mathematicians, computer scientists, and others cooperating in its development. I'm always happy to see the artificial boundaries between academic disciplines crossed in this cooperative way. When they are, it seems new ideas and new intellectual breakthroughs inevitably follow. I'm hopeful that more philosophers, theologians, and everyday seekers and laypersons will enter the fray. I'm confident that when they do, they will find fertile ground for developing new models of God, new ways of contemplating the Divine, and new ways for thinking about the nature of life, the soul, and what it means to be a child of God.

8
THE TRUTH SHALL
SET YOU FREE

*For my own part, I consider it as nothing less than a
question of freedom or slavery. And in proportion to
the magnitude of the subject, ought to be the
freedom of the debate.
It is only in this way that we can hope to arrive at truth, and
fulfill the great responsibility which we hold to God.*

—Patrick Henry, 1775[1]

In the previous chapters, we have made some general observations, raised a few issues or potential issues, kicked around some ideas, played with some concepts, and hopefully had a little fun while opening our minds to some new ideas and ways of thinking about technology and spirituality. Each chapter has examined our relationship with technology through what I've occasionally referred to as a "lens." We've used seven of these lenses so far, and I have given each a one-word name in order to make them easier to remember.

In this chapter, we'll look through the eighth and final lens, which I have given the name "liberty." Arguably, it's the most important, and the one that is perhaps the most value-laden, the one that gives us the best handle on how we go about evaluating technologies in terms of their impact on our spiritual lives. As such, it's a good introduction to how we might use all eight lenses in an evaluative matrix, so the chapter will conclude with an overview of all eight lenses and how we might use them in doing what I've advocated from the start: namely, be selective about which technologies we use, careful about how we use them, and mindful as to how they affect us.

SELLING THE GOLDEN CALF

Technology makes a lot of promises. Sometimes it delivers; often it does not. On a practical level, the consequences are obvious: stuff works for us or it doesn't, we praise its products and benefits, bemoan its shortcomings and costs, or, usually, both. Technology is always developed to address some perceived want or need (even if, as is often the case, we don't know what that need or want is until after the fact), and we judge it by how well it meets that want or need. We listen to the promises with a critical ear—for we have been fooled before—and we judge how well those promises are fulfilled by how readily the technology is adopted and how much people are willing to pay for it, financially and otherwise.

On a spiritual level the process is similar, but the promises made are often less transparent, less obvious, or at least less overt. Technologists will make rather bold claims on the practical side ("the Acme KXG-347 hyperwidget will triple your ferndale capital product ratio in three weeks or less") but seldom on the spiritual ("unlimited minutes in the divine presence on nights and weekends"). Still, those promises are there. It just takes a little more interpretation to tease them out.

We're all familiar with the way messages are hidden in advertisements. Take the typical television ad for an automobile. While the words spoken mention price, features, quality, and specifications such as horsepower, acceleration, gas mileage, and so on, the images and music carry the real message, typically about things like sex, power, status, youth, or lost youth (note the dominance of "classic" rock in ads these days). They don't always come right out and say, "this car will improve your love life, take inches off your waist, make your boss respect you, and set your soul free," but the message is pretty clear just the same.

One of the most brilliant recent examples of technology marketing has been for Apple's iPod.[2] The ads don't even bother boring us with technical details; they just tell us what we want to hear: buy this product and you will be so cool you'll barely be able to stand it. Successful technology marketing depends upon an appeal to our most cherished values, and there are few things we value more than cool. But if advertisers want to hit you where you feel it most, sooner or later they are going to get around to appealing to your spiritual values.

GIVE ME LIBERTY

So what are your spiritual values? These can be hard to articulate, but when you try, there are a few words that might come immediately to mind. *Liberty* has to be somewhere near the top of my personal list. Of course, *truth, love,* and *beauty* all trump liberty, but as I said before, those are just other names for God. I think what the iPod ads promise even more overtly than cool is freedom—an unabashed, liberating enthusiasm for life so pure, so raw, that we can't help but dance.

In my religious tradition, we are sometimes admonished to be "slaves of/for/to Christ." We can find some of the biblical basis for this rather shocking language in Paul's letters to the Romans, where he says they have been "enslaved to God" (Romans 6:22, NRSV), and to the Corinthians, where he says they were "bought with a price" (1 Corinthians 6:20, NRSV). The fact that the distinction between "slave" and the more politically correct "servant" would not exist for a first-century reader clouds the issue a bit, but the message remains the same. Bob Dylan reminds us of it with his refrain, "you're gonna have to serve somebody."[3] What I gather both Bob and Paul (especially in the context of the Romans passage) are saying is that we're all slaves to someone or something. Whether you buy that or not, Jesus himself said that we can only serve one master (Matthew 6:24; Luke 16:13), so when Christians say they are slaves to Christ, what they're really saying is that they refuse to be a slave to anyone or anything else. It's a bold claim.

Of course, I need not appeal to the New Testament to lift up liberty as a core spiritual value. The central story of the Torah (the Jewish sacred text, composed of the five books of Moses) is one of liberation. Exodus, the second book of the Hebrew Bible (the "Old Testament" to Christians), tells the story of Moses leading the people out of slavery in Egypt, a tale that is clearly symbolic of our spiritual condition. Buddhism would seem at first blush to be fairly contemptuous of such petty attachments as personal freedom, but in another light its central teachings can be viewed as a process of liberation from the prisons we construct in our minds, built with bricks and bars formed of desire and expectation.

And so it goes. I'll not be so bold as to claim that liberty is an essential spiritual value in every religious tradition, but the desire for freedom is so basic to the human condition that I would be surprised if it wasn't. I will be so bold as to claim that liberty is a spiritual value that technology often appeals to and also, ironically, one that it most threatens.

How so? Cell phones claim to give us the freedom to go anywhere we choose, whenever we choose, while still staying in touch. MP3 players let us do the same, while still allowing us to listen to all our tunes. Can anything ever compare to that feeling of total liberation when you got your driver's license, or sat behind the wheel of your first car, no longer dependent on friends or family to take you where you wanted to go? The Internet frees us to "go" anywhere we want in cyberspace; to communicate with nearly anyone we want, anywhere in the world; to explore places we never knew existed; to seek knowledge from blogs and websites that our would-be oppressors would keep from us, if it were up to them.[4]

Perhaps nowhere has there been greater liberation than what has been taking place in the entertainment industry. Thanks to the digitization of content, we're now free to watch just about any movie ever made, listen to any song ever recorded, wherever and whenever we want. Remember when you had to wait until a specific time on a specific day to watch your favorite show? And then you were at the mercy of advertisers with their relentless commercials. Thank God for TiVo!

But is this freedom? Is being free to watch whatever movie you want, whenever you want to watch it, what Moses had in mind when he petitioned Pharaoh (Exodus 5:1 ff)?

KICKING THE HABIT

Technology really can be a liberating force. I guess that's why I like it so much. Of course, it can also be a tool of the oppressors, but that's a political issue. What need concern us in terms of our spirituality is how readily we oppress *ourselves*, how easily we come to depend on technology, and how, in turn, that dependence can lead to addiction.

Addiction is a form of slavery. If you have ever been truly addicted to something—cigarettes are a good example that many of us can relate to—then you know how true that is. When I still smoked, I liked to think I was in control of my life, but in reality much of my daily routine revolved around cigarettes and being somewhere I could smoke. (When I was in college, we smoked in class; how much harder it must be for smokers today.) And if I didn't always have enough money to pay the rent or buy groceries, I always managed to have cigarettes around. If I ever doubted who was really in control, all I had to do was try to quit. Which I did. Repeatedly.[5]

But isn't it a stretch to compare a truly addictive substance, like nicotine, alcohol, or heroin, to mere technology, like a cell phone or a Web browser? I don't think so, and I don't make the claim lightly. I've had some experience with addiction, and I think the comparison is both fair and apt. A good friend who was studying to become an addictions counselor once told me that clinical addiction is defined by *effect, dependence,* and *tolerance.* I think that's a pretty useful definition, even if it's not perfect or universally accepted. It's pretty strict and disqualifies a lot of things that tend to be called addiction, which is a word that, like *community* and *virtual,* suffers from overapplication to the point where its usefulness is threatened. Addiction is a serious thing, and it should not be trivialized by applying the term to anything from a harmless habit to a casual attraction. To be addicted to something—presumably a drug, but of course the notion of addiction can and has been applied usefully to all sorts of other destructive behaviors—that something must first have a mind-altering effect on us. Hence, if people claim to be addicted to gambling, they first have to believe that gambling has a mind-altering effect on them, which it clearly does for some people.

There's little doubt in my mind that technology can have a mind-altering effect on us. Just watch a toddler in front of a television or a teenager playing video games if you need convincing. Of course, the real test requires that you look inside your own mind, which can be difficult to do. Drug addicts are usually acutely aware of the mind-altering effects of their drug of choice; it's why they chose it, but sometimes the effects are pretty subtle or easily denied. I know cigarettes affected my mood and attitude, but not every smoker would agree. Of course, not every smoker is an addict either. Does having a cell phone have a mind-altering effect on you? A computer? An iPod? I don't ask these questions rhetorically.

The first step in determining whether a technology is becoming an addiction, and therefore enslaving you and stealing your liberty, is clarifying whether it has a mind-altering effect on you. The answer may well be "no." But if your cell phone makes you feel more secure, then I would say it has a mind-altering effect. Okay, it isn't heroin, and we haven't even established it as an addiction (yet), but it might, arguably, be having an effect on you. The same can be said for any number of useful and otherwise harmless gadgets.

Of course, that doesn't make them bad. "Feeling secure" isn't a bad thing, normally, and lots of mind-altering behaviors, like some drugs, have beneficial, or at least benign, effects. Many people consider the effects of caffeine beneficial, and many people find alcohol a harmless social lubricant. But can anyone with an ounce of integrity deny that these substances have mind-altering effects or are potentially addictive? The important thing is that we consider carefully what effect, if any, a given technology has on our mental state and that we remain open and honest enough with ourselves to be aware of an effect if there is one. That's not easy. Denial is typically a strong ingredient in any addiction.

Second, in order for something to be a true addiction, we need to see some indication of *tolerance;* that is, we need to observe a need for more of the thing, whether it's a drug or something else, in order to achieve the desired effect. This requirement eliminates a lot of things that we might otherwise consider addictions, separating addiction from mere dependence (which may not be desirable, but doesn't rise to the level of addiction and bondage). If carrying a cell phone makes me feel secure now, but a month from now I need to carry two cell phones to feel as secure, and a month after that, three, and so on, then I'm building up a tolerance. This is silly, of course, but if you find your cell phone usage increasing steadily over time, if the warm and fuzzy feeling you used to get from your one-hundred-minute-per-month plan is gone and you keep trying to get it back by going to five hundred or a thousand minutes per month, or if you like having a computer in your home but find yourself spending more and more time in front of it every year, then you might want to think about this for a bit.

Finally, there's the obvious: for something to be an addiction, we must be dependent on it. If we can "give it up anytime we want," then it isn't a true addiction. It may be a habit, it may be destructive, but it isn't an addiction unless there is some sense that we *need* it, that we can't function well without it. I would say a lot of technologies fit the bill on that score. And with most addictions, dependence develops over time and often comes slowly. We may start out using something, like a cell phone, as a clear choice or option, but eventually find we are afraid or even incapable of leaving home without it. How easy would it be for you to give up your PC, your telephone, your automobile, or your television?

I would argue that many of us are addicted to any number of technologies and that we should find this at least a little disturbing. Addiction by itself is not an indictment, but it should give us pause. I admit to being addicted to coffee, but I'm not terribly worried about it. If I felt the need, I believe I could quit, since I've done so before. But I'm not so sure I could give up television as easily, and the issue is complicated by the fact that I don't really want to. That said, I'm not sure it's a true addiction, or even if it is all that harmful. I remember reading about a study that determined a number of Europeans to be alcoholics, but so practiced at moderation that the social and medical effects of their condition were entirely benign. Could my addiction (if it is an addiction) to television be as benign, or is it a form of bondage that interferes with my spirituality? If I conclude that I'm not addicted to television, am I merely "in denial"? If I take my spiritual condition seriously, then these are important questions to ask.

Like I said before, I love technology. I like the way it can level the playing field, creating new opportunities for the less advantaged, and I like the way it can free our minds, expand our horizons, allow us to become the more fully human beings God is calling us to be. But I also worry, both on a personal level as I struggle with my own addictions and on a corporate level as I see a society grown soft and increasingly subservient to the media and government, that we're allowing technology to make us less free.

I said at the outset that technology is part of what makes us human. But if we allow ourselves to fall into addiction, to become slavish consumers of media-generated drivel disguised as entertainment and sensationalized, conjectural, ill-informed speculation disguised as news; if we can't spend more than a few waking minutes alone in our own skin; if we wouldn't know how to get through a day without being distracted by an army of microcomputer-embedded toys flashing and beeping and sending familiar "tunes" into our sexy, white earbuds, then we have sacrificed the very humanity we sought.

Technology has the power to liberate or enslave us. It can allow us to become more fully human, or it can rob us of our humanity. The choice is often ours. Remember the Israelites who wanted to go back to Egypt, who said they were better off under Pharaoh's control (Exodus 16:3)? Those people are still with us. Heck, they *are* us. Don't forget that, and be careful of what your friends ask you to try.

RETAKING THE RED PILL

The eight lenses I've tried to develop in this book form what can be thought of as an evaluative matrix. The basic idea is that to build up an accurate image of our relationship with technology or the relationship between technology and our spirituality, it's helpful to look at it from a number of different angles. Each "lens" of the matrix helps us to do just that, to think about the relationship from a unique angle or perspective. I like the idea of a lens because it implies focus, the way you might focus a microscope or a pair of binoculars on a given object. By adjusting the focus to a certain setting, things pop into view that you couldn't see or didn't notice before. Naturally, if you focus on one thing you de-focus on others, and that's the whole point of the matrix. No one lens tells the whole story, hence we try to apply the whole *matrix,* not just one lens or one mind-set, in order to construct as complete and accurate an impression as possible of how technology affects our spiritual lives.

It's important to note that the lenses are not absolute and that they often cross over. For example, much of chapter 3 about community worked with the idea that technology "annihilates time and space." Perhaps it occurred to you that this discussion of time and space belonged in chapter 6, on velocity. Indeed, it would have been appropriate there, but it came up for me when I was thinking about how the information revolution is changing the way we build and maintain community. The important thing is that we ask questions and make observations, not which "lens" we use. The lenses are merely devices for helping us to come up with questions and open our minds to what we see before us.

We were introduced to the lens I call "boundary" in the introduction. This lens pervades the text, really. In some respects, all of the chapters use it. The whole idea that technology and spirituality have a relationship grows out of an application of the boundary lens. Without it, we can safely leave our technology over here and spirituality over there and not worry ourselves with what one has to do with the other. They are completely separate things, after all. But what if they're not; what if they *do* affect each other; what if we have a spiritual relationship with our computers and a technical relationship with our religion? We might have to write a book about it.

The boundary lens came into play again when we talked about how we relate to our machines in chapters 4 and 5. Normally, we put pretty strong boundaries between living and nonliving, between animate beings and inanimate things, but what if we suspended our belief in those boundaries long enough to anthropomorphize our machines? Maybe that will allow us to have a more (mutually?) beneficial relationship with them. And what if we consider the possibility that our machines can be intelligent or even sentient? Might that give us a better understanding of ourselves? Of God? Of our own spirituality? I think so.

Chapter 1 introduced the simplicity lens, the idea that we consider our technology while being mindful of the notion of simplicity as a spiritual value or ideal. Simplicity has a strong qualitative overtone, and generally I think it helps us to look for those characteristics in our technology that are most congruent with a spiritual way of life. The simplicity lens is perhaps the easiest one to understand and the simplest to apply. When we think about how a technology affects us spiritually, we might ask, "How simple is it? How easily and smoothly does it integrate with my life? Does it have a harmonious and uncomplicated elegance to its working? Do function and form come together in an effortless, even obvious or "natural," way, or does it feel clunky, out of place, unnecessarily complicated, or just plain ugly?" These are highly subjective, aesthetic, even difficult (*simple* doesn't mean *easy*) questions, but they're some of the most important.

Chapter 2 gave us the transparency lens. The transparency lens is probably even easier to apply than the simplicity lens. It is like simplicity, and often they go together, but they are essentially different. Transparency, as the name implies, asks how "invisible" a technology is. Can we easily ignore it as we use it to do whatever it is we use it to do, or do we have to spend a lot of time fiddling with it or figuring it out? Does it attract a lot of attention to itself, forcing us to concentrate on it, or does it free us to focus our entire attention on the task at hand?

"Simple" technology is often pretty transparent, but it can be quite beautiful too. Some technologies are just so wonderfully elegant and beautiful you can't help but notice and admire them, like a fine woodworking tool that you look forward to using just because it works so well in such a seemingly effortless, simple way. A transparent technology, on the other hand, might actually be pretty ugly, but you don't care because you hardly notice it; you forget it's even there. Often that's exactly what you need from a technology: so much transparency that you don't even have to think about it as a technology. Transparency is the most important aspect of technology for technophobes, and a little technophobia is probably good for all of us.

Transparency is something I always look for in well-designed technology. A telephone that is comfortable to use, lets you hear the other person clearly, and doesn't require any additional input from you once you've placed the call is an example of good transparency. Computers are not nearly as transparent now as they soon will be.

There is an insidious side to transparency, though. In writing about how computers are changing us, MIT sociologist Sherry Turkle says the oft-touted "transparency" in software design implies an ignorance of how things work. She calls this "epistemic opacity," and fears it will encourage us to take things at "interface value" rather than probing below the surface to see what's really going on.[6] This is a good reminder that transparency, like all of the lenses of the matrix, is value neutral; it's there to get us to ask questions and is not just a quality where more (or less) is necessarily better.

In chapter 3, we talked about community and how the information revolution is revolutionizing how we build and think about communities. Community is also one of the lenses of the matrix. To apply it, we merely think about community and how a given technology affects our experience of and relationship to it. Most of us would consider community an essential ingredient in a spiritual life, and there's perhaps no other area where the information revolution is having greater impact.

Chapters 4 and 5 dealt with the idea of identity, which is our fifth lens of the matrix. Identity forked into two chapters because we had to consider both how our technology affects our sense of identity and how advances in artificial intelligence encourage (I would say require) us to consider the possibility that our machines also have an identity. So the identity lens really asks us to examine our machines in terms of the questions "Who am I?" and "Who are you?" Both are the starting points of the question "What is our relationship?" which is sort of where we started with all this. So the identity lens is what computer programmers call "recursive," something that loops back on itself. But since we're already using an optical metaphor, we could also think of this recursive nature as having sort of a "hall of mirrors" effect; we use the identity lens to examine our relationship with technology and to reflect back ourselves and our technology. This hall of mirrors effect might lead to the sort of mind-bending disorientation we sometimes need in order to begin to see things as they really are instead of as how we expect them to be.

The sixth lens is velocity, which, appropriately enough, came up in chapter 6. Using this lens we ask questions like

"How does this technology dominate my time? Does it allow me to live more fully in the present, or does it force or encourage me to focus too much of my attention on other places or times? Does it make my life more frantic, or does it allow my body and my soul to live in the same space? Does it whisk me away from those uncomfortable realities I need to confront, or does it allow, or even force, me to spend time in my own skin and in the divine presence?"

Chapter 7 gave us my favorite lens, connectivity. Through it we examine the connections that define our reality. Through it we begin to see how information and computer technology model, resemble, and perhaps reflect the true nature of the world and of God. Through the connectivity lens, we see the power of the network and the magic of the Web.

The connectivity lens is perhaps the most nebulous and the most difficult to apply of the eight lenses. It takes us to places and asks us to look at things most of us can barely begin to comprehend, let alone understand. On the other hand, it's pretty simple at its starting point. We simply think about a given technology in terms of the connections it provides and/or how it enables or affects our ability to make and maintain those connections. It can be as simple as noticing how many people you have established connections with by virtue of having a cell phone, thinking about the nature of those connections and how they might be different if you altered your behavior with or attitude toward your cell phone, what other connections might be affected or eliminated by your decisions, and so on. It's really quite flexible, and unlike some of the other lenses it's probably less oriented toward making value judgments about technologies (i.e., deciding whether or not a technology is good or bad for you) and more oriented toward making modifications in your attitude and behavior toward or with a given technology, though of course the entire matrix is intended as an evaluative tool for doing both.

And, finally, that brings us to where we started this chapter, with liberty. Like boundary, liberty also pervades the entire text. Addiction has come up several times throughout the book, and all of the chapters, and lenses, for that matter, serve to encourage our consideration of the overarching question "Does this technology free me to be myself, to be the fully human being that God is calling me to be, to live in better relationship with the Divine and with my fellow humans, or does it ultimately leave me in bondage?" If there's a way of summarizing the point of this entire exercise I suppose that might be it: that we endeavor to come up with some sort of informed and considered answer to that very difficult question. If I have succeeded in getting you to ask it, our time spent together has been worthwhile. If this book has been of any help in your deliberations, I have achieved my goal, and if you come up with an answer, please share it with me. We're all in this together, after all.

NOTES

CHAPTER 0: REDEFINING THE BOUNDARIES

1. I say "help *us*" rather than "help *you*" or "help *the reader*" because we are in this together. I can only hope that those who read this book will learn a fraction of what I have learned writing it.

2. Roughly half my classes at Ball State were at the Teachers College and the rest were at the Center for Information and Communication Science (CICS). The differences between those two centers of learning were profound, but any extended discussion of them here would be a distraction. The Teachers College was certainly much more open to the humanities, but it was primarily driven by the social sciences—with the emphasis on science—and while emerging technologies might be viewed as a personal challenge and an annoyance, the consensus view was fairly techtopian. At the CICS, technology was indeed supreme, and while it is no doubt an insult to the religiosity of the faculty and staff there to claim that technology is their god, their attitude toward information technology could certainly look a bit idolatrous to the uninitiated.

3. No relationship to the movie of the same title, I swear, but if you haven't seen the movie, don't waste time trying to make sense of the "red pill" reference.

4. This notion of boundary first came to me while I was hiking the Appalachian Trail along the Tennessee–North Carolina border, crossing back and forth from one state to the other often, sometimes literally with every step. The seemingly necessary notion of borders between nation-states disintegrates into meaninglessness in such a setting, where one is walking down a trail in the woods. This boundary, so important that you would be hard-pressed to find a map of the area that did not show it prominently, meant no more to me than it did to the bears.

   At one point, I lunched at the site of an old mountaintop hotel. The hotel was famous for being half in one state, half in the other, one state dry, the other wet. It seems there was a line painted on the floor of the ballroom corresponding to the legal boundary. Drinks were served on one side of the line, but police would arrest anyone who carried a drink onto the other. Sitting in that spot, now almost completely wild, the hotel having been torn down decades ago, led me to contemplate how real such boundaries can seem, worth killing and dying for in judgment of countless of my fellow human beings, and how absurd they seem when they have no real consequence in nature.

5. "Thinking outside the box" is an expression I've grown to detest. It seems to be most popular in environments where people who actually do it are punished for it. I actually prefer "coloring outside the lines," which is just as clichéd, but has a sense of the mischievous and suggests a certain recklessness and apparent incompetence truer to the outlaw nature of "out of the box" thinking.

6. Third in terms of the order in which they are presented here; the numbering is unimportant.

7. Douglas S. Robertson, *The New Renaissance: Computers and the Next Level of Civilization* (New York: Oxford University Press, 1998).

8. This chapter title is taken from Sammy Hagar's song of the same name, a 1984 single released by Geffen Records.

9. Rebecca Solnit, *River of Shadows: Eadweard Muybridge and the Technological Wild West* (San Francisco: Viking, 2003).

CHAPTER 1: 'TIS A GIFT TO BE SIMPLE

1. Classic Shaker work song. The first three lines comprise a second verse, written later than the epigraph suggests; it refers to the concluding refrain and the more familiar first verse, reflected in this chapter's title.

2. Whether or not Ned Ludd ever existed in the flesh, he achieved mythical status by the time the Luddites came into being.

3. *The Great War and the Shaping of the 20th Century.* First broadcast in 1996 as a KCET (PBS)/BBC co-production. See also http://www.pbs.org/greatwar/.

4. Edward Gibbon, *The Decline and Fall of the Roman Empire* (classic work, various publishers). See particularly chapters XV and XVI of this classic late eighteenth–century work.

5. Donald B. Kraybill and Marc A. Olshan, eds., *The Amish Struggle with Modernity* (Hanover, NH: University Press of New England, 1994), p. vii.

6. Howard Rheingold, "Look Who's Talking," *Wired,* January 1999.

7. Joshua Davis, "Come to LeBow Country," *Wired,* February 2003.

8. David Luthy, "Amish Migration Patterns: 1972–1992" (Appendix) in Donald B. Kraybill and Marc A. Olshan, eds., *The Amish Struggle with Modernity* (Hanover, NH: University Press of New England, 1994).

9. www.padutch.com/atafaq.shtml.

10. Edward Demming Andrews and Faith Andrews, *Work and Worship: The Economic Order of the Shakers* (Greenwich, CT: New York Graphic Society, 1974).

11. Ibid.

12. Doris Faber, *The Perfect Life: The Shakers in America* (New York: Farrar, Straus and Giroux, 1974), p. 119.

13. Ibid, p. 65.

14. Edward Demming Andrews, *Work and Worship*, p. 146.

CHAPTER 2: FINDING OUR WAY

1. Despite their near total domination of the computer market through the '70s, IBM got into the personal computer market late and missed out on most of the potential revenues because they, like virtually everyone else, underestimated the potential market for the PC, believing that only relatively few (and relatively poor) hobbyists would be interested in it. Apple was actually the first company to exploit the mass PC market, mainly by making the computer more "friendly," but later lost their advantage to Microsoft. For more on this, see Jim Carlton, *Apple: The Inside Story of Intrigue, Egomania, and Business Blunders* (New York: Random House, 1997).

2. I talked to Keith recently and he's come around on this point. He now asserts that he was mistaken to think of the computer as "just a tool." He now considers it "dangerous." Couldn't have said it better myself.

3. The notion that the advent of print changed the way we think and construct knowledge is perhaps best articulated by Marshall McLuhan in his classic and ingenious work *The Gutenberg Galaxy* (Toronto: University of Toronto Press, 1962), though countless others have made the case as well.

4. Bruce Springsteen, "57 Channels (And Nothin' On)," 1992. *Human Touch*, Sony/Columbia (ASCAP).

5. Bruce Schneier, *Beyond Fear: Thinking Sensibly About Security in an Uncertain World* (New York: Copernicus Books, 2003). Also see http://www.schneier.com.

CHAPTER 3: VIRTUAL VILLAGE

1. The Emerson quote is third-hand at best; I got it from Rebecca Solnit, *River of Shadows: Eadweard Muybridge and the Technological Wild West* (New York: Penguin, 2003), p. 11, who got it from John F. Kasson, *Civilizing the Machine* (New York: Grossman, 1976), p. 120, who, I can only hope, got it from Emerson.

2. If you find the idea of "shopping" for a religion a little unsettling, you're in good company. See Richard Cimino and Don Lattin, *Shopping for Faith: American Religion in the New Millennium* (San Francisco: Jossey Bass, 1998).

3. Just how secure is your privacy (or anything else for that matter) on the Internet? That is a huge question for our time, and the answer is in flux. But alas, these are political phenomena and well outside the scope of this book, so I must resist my urge to rant. See http://www.schneier.com for some good stuff though.

4. R.D. Putnam, *Bowling Alone: The Collapse and Revival of American Community* (New York: Simon & Schuster, 2000).

5. Geoff Nunberg, "On Community," radio essay. *Fresh Air with Terry Gross*, WHYY-FM/National Public Radio, September 27, 2000. Hopefully you can still find it archived at http://www.freshair.npr.org.

6. George Wood, *Let's Talk About Community: A Discussion of Multiple Communities Theory*, draft ed. (Muncie, IN: Ball State University, 1998).

7. Neil Gershenfeld, "Cyberspace Is Dead," in *Wired*, February 2006. He suggests "the world" as a replacement term, saying, "Information technologies are finally growing up, so we can interact with them in our world instead of theirs." See also http://www.endofcyberspace.com/.

8. *The Matrix*, DVD, directed by Andy and Larry Wachowski (Warner Brothers, 1999). The quoted line comes in scene 12 (DVD) when Morpheus first explains the Matrix to Neo.

9. William Irwin, *The Matrix and Philosophy: Welcome to the Desert of the Real* (La Salle, IL: Open Court, 2002). This explores some of the arguments and issues.

10. Max Tegmark, "Parallel Universes," in *Scientific American*, May 2003 (also available in a 2004 "Special Report" reprint).

11. See René Descartes, *Discourse on the Method of Rightly Directing One's Reason and of Seeking Truth in the Sciences*, typically called "the Discourse" originally published in 1637, or his *Meditations on First Philosophy*, published somewhat later. Numerous translations

are widely available. Descartes, you will no doubt recall, is famous for his epistemological jumping-off point, "cogito ergo sum." (I am thinking, therefore I exist.) Donald Palmer gives a thorough and entertaining summary of Descartes' (and nearly every other major European philosopher's) arguments in *Does the Center Hold? An Introduction to Western Philosophy* (Mountain View, CA: Mayfield, 1991).

12. Rena M. Palloff and Keith Pratt, *Building Learning Communities in Cyberspace: Effective Strategies for the Online Classroom* (San Francisco, Jossey-Bass, 1999).

13. Rebecca Solnit, *River of Shadows: Eadweard Muybridge and the Technological Wild West* (New York: Penguin, 2003).

14. Thomas Friedman, *The World Is Flat: A Brief History of the Twenty-first Century* (New York: Farrar, Straus and Giroux, 2005).

CHAPTER 4: I AM MY IPOD

1. James Yerkes, "As Good as It Gets: The Religious Consciousness in John Updike's Literary Vision," in James Yerkes, ed., *John Updike and Religion: The Sense of the Sacred and the Motions of Grace* (Grand Rapids, MI: Eerdmans, 1999), p. 27.

2. Jennifer Cobb, *Cybergrace: The Search for God in the Digital World* (New York: Crown, 1998), p. 20.

3. Henry Petroski, *To Engineer Is Human: The Role of Failure in Successful Design* (New York: St. Martins Press, 1985).

4. Philip Hefner has written a beautiful and concise series of lectures on how technology is intimately a part of the process of becoming in *Technology and Human Becoming* (Minneapolis: Fortress Press, 2003).

5. Jack Mezirow and Associates, *Learning as Transformation: Critical Perspectives on a Theory in Progress* (San Francisco: Jossey-Bass, 2000).

6. This and the previous heading are taken from David Bowie's "Changes," 1972. *Hunky Dory*, RCA.

7. I was still a kid when my eyes were opened by Alvin Toffler's *Future Shock* (New York: Random House, 1970). For a bio, see http://leighbureau.com/speaker.asp?id=17.

8. *2001: A Space Odyssey*, directed by Stanley Kubrick (MGM, 1968).

9. Mae and Ira Freeman, *You Will Go to the Moon* (New York: Beginners Books, 1959). You can read several reviews at Amazon.com that support my thesis.

10. There have been some pretty dramatic improvements in infrastructure in that century, most recently the use of fiber optic technology for long lines and a digital system (SS-7) for routing calls, but the "last mile" of line between your home and the network is only now beginning to be upgraded, and it remains to be seen whether or when this will ever reach us yokels out here in the sticks. And I really do think the sound quality and clarity of telephone communication has deteriorated dramatically lately, due in most part to the poor-quality phones we're using.

11. Actually, I've oversimplified if not misstated Moore's Law here, but not substantially and in the usual way. See the Wikipedia (http://en.wikipedia.org) entry for Moore's Law for a good overview of what it really is and what it means.

12. "Bugs" sounds so much cuter than "defects," which is what they really are, but this is not marketing spin; code defects have always been known as bugs so far as I know, and they are a guaranteed part of the development process. Part of the reason they're known as bugs is that they hide so well. One of the hardest parts of debugging code is finding out that the bugs exist in the first place. This is where software consumers can play a big role, since they are the ones who are really going to put the program through its paces performing real-world tasks. Unfortunately, the way the market is set up, this potentially valuable feedback loop often gets inhibited by the developers' reluctance to admit fault. That said, software developers are not stupid, and lately you will notice a lot of software comes with some mechanism for easily reporting bugs and crashes.

13. There are exceptions, of course. Some upgrades are little more than bug fixes and patches and will not upset your established practices or stress you out in any way. Open source software developers are particularly good at issuing regular updates and upgrades that do not subject you to marketing-driven changes and feature creep. For example, I heartily recommend the Firefox Web browser, available free from www.mozilla.org, and I further recommend that you update it regularly; there is virtually no reason not to. A good rule of thumb might be that if the upgrade is free, you probably want it—it may contain important patches and security updates; if it costs money, *caveat emptor* (classically translated as "let the buyer beware," but what it really implies is that you need to know what you are buying and should not trust the seller to tell you).

14. I have always hated the term *netiquette*, and now I know why (aside from a general distaste for puns). We shouldn't create special terms for things done online. Etiquette is etiquette, regardless of where you

are. Rules and conventions of politeness may be different online and off-line, just as being polite at your grandmother's tea party would look different than being polite at your little brother's kegger, but it's still being polite; it didn't become something different just because you are in a different social setting.

15. Most of our online classes at ESR and Bethany had some "face time" component, and accreditation requirements precluded anyone from graduating without taking a lot of face-to-face classes. That may have helped reassure the faculty, but I've seen some pretty questionable people get through the process, and I think it's a lot harder to "hide" long-term online than it is in a conventional seminary setting. I predict the day will come when we stand this requirement on its head and insist that all seminarians take at least some online courses, for fear we would never discover the true person otherwise.

16. Many MMORPGs are fantasy-based, and hence you are likely to be an elf or a troll or some other invented creature, or at least have magical powers.

17. Marshall McLuhan, *Understanding Media: The Extensions of Man* (New York: Times Mirror, 1964).

CHAPTER 5: ARIGATO, ROBOTO

1. *Serenity,* directed by Joss Whedon (Universal City, CA: Universal Studios, 2005), closing lines.

2. *Firefly,* directed by Joss Whedon (Beverly Hills, CA: Twentieth Century Fox, 2002). The series consists of fourteen episodes, including three that never aired and the two-hour pilot, which aired only after the series had been canceled. Whedon is more famous for one of his other shows, *Buffy the Vampire Slayer* (Beverly Hills, CA: Twentieth Century Fox, 1997), which is way better than you think it will be. Both are available on DVD.

3. "Out of Gas," *Firefly,* directed by Joss Whedon (Beverly Hills, CA: Twentieth Century Fox, 2002), original air date Oct. 25, 2002.

4. Ibid.

5. I really love Orson Scott Card's playful exploration of knacks in his "Tales of Alvin Maker" series, beginning with *Seventh Son* (New York: Tom Doherty Associates, 1987), and I have to credit him for much of my thinking along these lines. These books are neither fantasy nor science fiction. They are essentially historical novels, but Card's alternate history is also alternate reality in terms of the role of magic. In Alvin's world, magic is center stage and an important

aspect of daily life on the early nineteenth–century American frontier. Card gives it a realistic flavor though, and half convinces you the magical world of his imagination really could have existed had our ancestors been less hostile to witchcraft and paid more attention to the small miracles in their, and by implication our, daily lives.

6. *2001: A Space Odyssey,* directed by Stanley Kubrick (MGM, 1968).

7. Mary Shelley, *Frankenstein; or, The Modern Prometheus,* 1818 (classic work, various publishers).

CHAPTER 6: I CAN'T DRIVE 55

1. David Zindell, *Neverness* (New York: Bantam, 1988), pp. 393–394. Quite possibly the best science fiction novel I've ever read.

2. See chapter 4, note 10 on Moore's Law.

CHAPTER 7: NEUTRONS, NETWORKS, AND NEW MODELS OF GOD

1. Richard Feynman, *The Character of Physical Law* (New York: Random House, 1965), p. 52.

2. Sallie McFague, *Models of God: Theology for an Ecological, Nuclear Age* (Minneapolis, MN: Augsburg Fortress, 1987).

3. For the role of math in physics, see Feynman, *The Character of Physical Law,* particularly the second lecture (chapter), "The Relation of Mathematics to Physics." For a closer look at the author, a deeply spiritual atheist who refused to believe in a god smaller than his experience of the world, I recommend James Gleick, *Genius: The Life and Science of Richard Feynman* (New York: Random House, 1992).

4. Since, in the final analysis, all things *are* connected, the notion of *feeling* connected to the world, to each other, and to God is a false one. We either are connected (to everything) or we're not; *feeling* connected to one and not to another is a delusion, or perhaps a disease. Of course, that says nothing about the quality and nature of those connections, a topic of endless speculation and concern.

5. It irks me to say this, since the whole foundation for my research approach on the Appalachian Trail was that it is silly to try to quantify either technology or spirituality, but if you don't read too much into it, this statement is essentially in keeping with my research findings.

6. Battery technology is one of the biggest hurdles to be overcome in the consumer electronics industry; when we solve that little problem,

things will really start to move forward, but so far it has been an exceedingly intransigent problem. Today's batteries are only marginally better than the ones your grandparents used as children.

7. "Foreseeable future" always strikes me as an oxymoron, but it's hard to imagine anything substantially unlike a PC supplanting its current station in the consumer consciousness as the symbolic focal point of the information revolution. Though the PC's ultimate demise is inevitable, it seems at least probable that, rather than being replaced, it will gradually morph into something sufficiently removed from its primitive forerunners to the point where we'll have to call it by another name.

8. http://setiathome.berkeley.edu/

9. Duncan J. Watts, *Six Degrees: The Science of a Connected Age* (New York: W. W. Norton, 2003).

CHAPTER 8: THE TRUTH SHALL SET YOU FREE

1. William Wirt, *Sketches of the Life and Character of Patrick Henry* (Philadelphia: James Webster, 1817), p. 120. Verb tenses changed by author. Obtained online from the digital collections of the University of North Carolina at Chapel Hill, http://docsouth.unc.edu/southlit/wirt/wirt.html.

2. Steven Levy, *The Perfect Thing: How the iPod Shuffles Commerce, Culture, and Coolness* (New York: Simon & Schuster, 2006).

3. Bob Dylan, "Gotta Serve Somebody," 1979. *Slow Train Coming,* Special Rider Music.

4. Keep an eye on what's going on with Internet access in China to understand some of the issues here, and an even closer eye on telecommunications policies in the United States, which threaten to change the open nature of the Internet. See especially the writings of Lawrence Lessig, e.g., *The Future of Ideas: The Fate of the Commons in a Connected World* (New York: Random House, 2001).

5. I smoked my last cigarette on July 31, 1989, but I'm still a nicotine addict. Quitting was the hardest thing I ever did, and the only thing that keeps me from smoking today is the near certain knowledge that I wouldn't be able to quit again. Yet some people find it easy. As they say in Alcoholics Anonymous, "some of us are sicker than others."

6. Sherry Turkle, "How Computers Change the Way We Think," in *The Chronicle Review* 50, no. 21 (2004):B26.

SUGGESTIONS FOR FURTHER READING

Throughout this project I have been struck with what an audacious undertaking it is to write a book, as if what one person has to say is worthy of another's considerable investment of time and money. But alas, humility comes too late sometimes, and I've never been very good at keeping my mouth shut when I'm passionate about something. In that particular defect of character at least I'm in good company; there are countless similarly passionate, if not audacious, people out there whose wisdom on the various topics I've approached in this short book exceeds my own by many orders of magnitude. Some of these people have been cited, and I encourage you to peruse the endnotes. That said, a little redundancy never hurts, and I have listed just a few of what I think may be the more entertaining and accessible books here, as well as a few others that have informed me along the way even though they were not cited specifically.

ON THE AMISH AND SHAKERS

Andrews, Edward Deming, and Faith Andrews. *Work and Worship: The Economic Order of the Shakers.* Greenwich, CT: New York Graphic Society, 1974.

Kraybill, Donald B., and Marc A. Olshan, eds. *The Amish Struggle with Modernity.* Hanover, NH: University Press of New England, 1994.

ON TECHNOLOGY AND RELIGION

Beaudoin, Tom. *Virtual Faith: The Irreverent Spiritual Quest of Generation X.* San Francisco: Jossey-Bass, 1998.

Brasher, Brenda E. *Give Me That Online Religion.* San Francisco: Jossey-Bass, 2001.

Cobb, Jennifer. *CyberGrace: The Search for God in the Digital World.* New York: Crown, 1998.

Hammerman, Joshua. *Thelordismyshepherd.com: Seeking God in Cyberspace.* Deerfield Beach, FL: Simcha Press, 2000.

Hefner, Philip. *Technology and Human Becoming.* Minneapolis: Fortress Press, 2003.

Hipps, Shane. *The Hidden Power of Electronic Culture: How Media Shapes Faith, the Gospel, and Church*. Grand Rapids, MI: Zondervan, 2005.

ON TECHNOLOGY AND CULTURE

Friedman, Thomas. *The World Is Flat: A Brief History of the Twenty-first Century*. New York: Farrar, Straus and Giroux, 2005.

Lessig, Lawrence. *The Future of Ideas: The Fate of the Commons in a Connected World*. New York: Random House, 2001.

McLuhan, Marshall. *Understanding Media: The Extensions of Man*. New York: Times Mirror, 1964.

Naisbitt, John. *High Tech, High Touch: Technology and Our Search for Meaning*. New York: Broadway Books, 1999.

Robertson, Douglas S. *The New Renaissance: Computers and the Next Level of Civilization*. New York: Oxford University Press, 1998.

Solnit, Rebecca. *River of Shadows: Eadweard Muybridge and the Technological Wild West*. New York: Viking, 2003.

ON SCIENCE, PHYSICS, AND NETWORKS

Barbour, Ian. *When Science Meets Religion*. San Francisco: HarperSanFrancisco, 2000.

Feynman, Richard. *The Character of Physical Law*. New York: Random House, 1965.

Nelson, David. *Judaism, Physics and God: Searching for Sacred Metaphors in a Post-Einstein World*. Woodstock, VT: Jewish Lights Publishing, 2005.

Watts, Duncan J. *Six Degrees: The Science of a Connected Age*. New York: Norton, 2003.

ON WALKING AND THE APPALACHIAN TRAIL

Bryson, Bill. *A Walk in the Woods: Rediscovering America on the Appalachian Trail*. New York: Broadway Books, 1998.

Emblidge, David, ed. *The Appalachian Trail Reader*. New York: Oxford University Press, 1996.

Solnit, Rebecca. *Wanderlust: A History of Walking*. New York: Viking, 2000.

FOR JUST PLAIN FUN READING (FICTION)
WHERE TECHNOLOGY AND SPIRITUALITY COEXIST

Card, Orson Scott. *Seventh Son*. New York: Tom Doherty Associates, 1987.

Zindell, David. *Neverness: A Novel*. New York: Bantam, 1988.

Global Spiritual Perspectives

Spiritual Perspectives on America's Role as Superpower

by the Editors at SkyLight Paths

Are we the world's good neighbor or a global bully? From a spiritual perspective, what are America's responsibilities as the only remaining superpower? Contributors: **Dr. Beatrice Bruteau • Dr. Joan Brown Campbell • Tony Campolo • Rev. Forrest Church • Lama Surya Das • Matthew Fox • Kabir Helminski • Thich Nhat Hanh • Eboo Patel • Abbot M. Basil Pennington, ocso • Dennis Prager • Rosemary Radford Ruether • Wayne Teasdale • Rev. William McD. Tully • Rabbi Arthur Waskow • John Wilson**

5½ x 8½, 256 pp, Quality PB, 978-1-893361-81-2 **$16.95**

Spiritual Perspectives on Globalization, 2nd Edition
Making Sense of Economic and Cultural Upheaval

by Ira Rifkin; Foreword by Dr. David Little, Harvard Divinity School

What is globalization? Surveys the religious landscape. Includes a new Discussion Guide designed for group use.

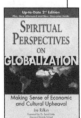

5½ x 8½, 256 pp, Quality PB, 978-1-59473-045-0 **$16.99**

Hinduism / Vedanta

The Four Yogas
A Guide to the Spiritual Paths of Action, Devotion, Meditation and Knowledge
by Swami Adiswarananda 6 x 9, 320 pp, HC, 978-1-59473-143-3 **$29.99**

Meditation & Its Practices
A Definitive Guide to Techniques and Traditions of Meditation in Yoga and Vedanta
by Swami Adiswarananda 6 x 9, 504 pp, Quality PB, 978-1-59473-105-1 **$19.99**

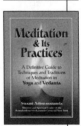

The Spiritual Quest and the Way of Yoga: The Goal, the Journey and the Milestones
by Swami Adiswarananda 6 x 9, 288 pp, HC, 978-1-59473-113-6 **$29.99**

Sri Ramakrishna, the Face of Silence
by Swami Nikhilananda and Dhan Gopal Mukerji
Edited with an Introduction by Swami Adiswarananda; Foreword by Dhan Gopal Mukerji II
Classic biographies present the life and thought of Sri Ramakrishna.
6 x 9, 352 pp, HC, 978-1-59473-115-0 **$29.99**

Sri Sarada Devi, The Holy Mother
Her Teachings and Conversations
Translated with Notes by Swami Nikhilananda; Edited with an Introduction by Swami Adiswarananda
6 x 9, 288 pp, HC, 978-1-59473-070-2 **$29.99**

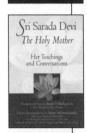

The Vedanta Way to Peace and Happiness *by Swami Adiswarananda*
6 x 9, 240 pp, HC, 978-1-59473-034-4 **$29.99**

Vivekananda, World Teacher: His Teachings on the Spiritual Unity of Humankind
Edited and with an Introduction by Swami Adiswarananda
6 x 9, 272 pp, Quality PB, 978-1-59473-210-2 **$21.99**

Sikhism

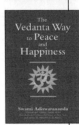

The First Sikh Spiritual Master
Timeless Wisdom from the Life and Teachings of Guru Nanak *by Harish Dhillon*
Tells the story of a unique spiritual leader who showed a gentle, peaceful path to God-realization while highlighting Guru Nanak's quest for tolerance and compassion. 6 x 9, 192 pp, Quality PB, 978-1-59473-209-6 **$16.99**

Or phone, fax, mail or e-mail to: SKYLIGHT PATHS Publishing
Sunset Farm Offices, Route 4 • P.O. Box 237 • Woodstock, Vermont 05091
Tel: (802) 457-4000 • Fax: (802) 457-4004 • www.skylightpaths.com
Credit card orders: (800) 962-4544 (8:30AM–5:30PM ET Monday–Friday)
Generous discounts on quantity orders. SATISFACTION GUARANTEED. Prices subject to change.

Spiritual Poetry—The Mystic Poets

Experience these mystic poets as you never have before. Each beautiful, compact book includes: a brief introduction to the poet's time and place; a summary of the major themes of the poet's mysticism and religious tradition; essential selections from the poet's most important works; and an appreciative preface by a contemporary spiritual writer.

   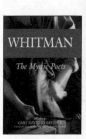

Hafiz: The Mystic Poets
Preface by Ibrahim Gamard
Hafiz is known throughout the world as Persia's greatest poet, with sales of his poems in Iran today only surpassed by those of the Qur'an itself. His probing and joyful verse speaks to people from all backgrounds who long to taste and feel divine love and experience harmony with all living things.
5 x 7¼, 144 pp, HC, 978-1-59473-009-2 **$16.99**

Hopkins: The Mystic Poets
Preface by Rev. Thomas Ryan, CSP
Gerard Manley Hopkins, Christian mystical poet, is beloved for his use of fresh language and startling metaphors to describe the world around him. Although his verse is lovely, beneath the surface lies a searching soul, wrestling with and yearning for God.
5 x 7¼, 112 pp, HC, 978-1-59473-010-8 **$16.99**

Tagore: The Mystic Poets
Preface by Swami Adiswarananda
Rabindranath Tagore is often considered the "Shakespeare" of modern India. A great mystic, Tagore was the teacher of W. B. Yeats and Robert Frost, the close friend of Albert Einstein and Mahatma Gandhi, and the winner of the Nobel Prize for Literature. This beautiful sampling of Tagore's two most important works, *The Gardener* and *Gitanjali,* offers a glimpse into his spiritual vision that has inspired people around the world.
5 x 7¼, 144 pp, HC, 978-1-59473-008-5 **$16.99**

Whitman: The Mystic Poets
Preface by Gary David Comstock
Walt Whitman was the most innovative and influential poet of the nineteenth century. This beautiful sampling of Whitman's most important poetry from *Leaves of Grass,* and selections from his prose writings, offers a glimpse into the spiritual side of his most radical themes—love for country, love for others, and love of Self.
5 x 7¼, 192 pp, HC, 978-1-59473-041-2 **$16.99**

Kabbalah from Jewish Lights Publishing

Awakening to Kabbalah: The Guiding Light of Spiritual Fulfillment
by Rav Michael Laitman, PhD 6 x 9, 192 pp, HC, 978-1-58023-264-7 **$21.99**

Cast in God's Image: Discover Your Personality Type Using the Enneagram and Kabbalah
by Rabbi Howard A. Addison 7 x 9, 176 pp, Quality PB, 978-1-58023-124-4 **$16.95**

Ehyeh: A Kabbalah for Tomorrow *by Dr. Arthur Green*
6 x 9, 224 pp, Quality PB, 978-1-58023-213-5 **$16.99**

The Enneagram and Kabbalah, 2nd Edition: Reading Your Soul
by Rabbi Howard A. Addison 6 x 9, 192 pp, Quality PB, 978-1-58023-229-6 **$16.99**

Finding Joy: A Practical Spiritual Guide to Happiness *by Dannel I. Schwartz with Mark Hass*
6 x 9, 192 pp, Quality PB, 978-1-58023-009-4 **$14.95**

The Gift of Kabbalah: Discovering the Secrets of Heaven, Renewing Your Life on Earth
by Tamar Frankiel, PhD 6 x 9, 256 pp, Quality PB, 978-1-58023-141-1 **$16.95**
HC, 978-1-58023-108-4 **$21.95**

Honey from the Rock: An Easy Introduction to Jewish Mysticism
by Lawrence Kushner 6 x 9, 176 pp, Quality PB, 978-1-58023-073-5 **$16.95**

Kabbalah: A Brief Introduction for Christians
by Tamar Frankiel, PhD 5½ x 8½, 176 pp, Quality PB, 978-1-58023-303-3 **$16.99**

Zohar: Annotated & Explained *Translation and Annotation by Dr. Daniel C. Matt*
Foreword by Andrew Harvey 5½ x 8½, 176 pp, Quality PB, 978-1-893361-51-5 **$15.99**

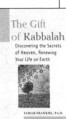
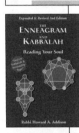

Judaism / Christianity

Christians and Jews in Dialogue: Learning in the Presence of the Other
by Mary C. Boys and Sara S. Lee; Foreword by Dorothy C. Bass
Inspires renewed commitment to dialogue between religious traditions and illuminates how it should happen. Explains the transformative work of creating environments for Jews and Christians to study together and enter the dynamism of the other's religious tradition.
6 x 9, 240 pp, HC, 978-1-59473-144-0 **$21.99**

Healing the Jewish-Christian Rift: Growing Beyond Our Wounded History
by Ron Miller and Laura Bernstein; Foreword by Dr. Beatrice Bruteau
6 x 9, 288 pp, Quality PB, 978-1-59473-139-6 **$18.99**

Introducing My Faith and My Community
The Jewish Outreach Institute Guide for the Christian in a Jewish Interfaith Relationship
by Rabbi Kerry M. Olitzky 6 x 9, 176 pp, Quality PB, 978-1-58023-192-3 **$16.99** *(a Jewish Lights book)*

The Jewish Approach to God: A Brief Introduction for Christians
by Rabbi Neil Gillman 5½ x 8½, 192 pp, Quality PB, 978-1-58023-190-9 **$16.95** *(a Jewish Lights book)*

Jewish Holidays: A Brief Introduction for Christians
by Rabbi Kerry M. Olitzky and Rabbi Daniel Judson
5½ x 8½, 176 pp, Quality PB, 978-1-58023-302-6 **$16.99** *(a Jewish Lights book)*

Jewish Ritual: A Brief Introduction for Christians
by Rabbi Kerry M. Olitzky and Rabbi Daniel Judson
5½ x 8½, 144 pp, Quality PB, 978-1-58023-210-4 **$14.99** *(a Jewish Lights book)*

Jewish Spirituality: A Brief Introduction for Christians
by Rabbi Lawrence Kushner
5½ x 8½, 112 pp, Quality PB, 978-1-58023-150-3 **$12.95** *(a Jewish Lights book)*

A Jewish Understanding of the New Testament
by Rabbi Samuel Sandmel; new Preface by Rabbi David Sandmel
5½ x 8½, 368 pp, Quality PB, 978-1-59473-048-1 **$19.99**

We Jews and Jesus
Exploring Theological Differences for Mutual Understanding
by Rabbi Samuel Sandmel; new Preface by Rabbi David Sandmel A Classic Reprint
Written in a non-technical way for the layperson, this candid and forthright look at the what and why of the Jewish attitude toward Jesus is a clear and forceful exposition that guides both Christians and Jews in relevant discussion.
6 x 9, 192 pp, Quality PB, 978-1-59473-208-9 **$16.99**

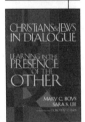

Sacred Texts—SkyLight Illuminations Series

Offers today's spiritual seeker an accessible entry into the great classic texts of the world's spiritual traditions. Each classic is presented in an accessible translation, with facing pages of guided commentary from experts, giving you the keys you need to understand the history, context and meaning of the text. This series enables you, whatever your background, to experience and understand classic spiritual texts directly, and to make them a part of your life.

CHRISTIANITY

The End of Days: Essential Selections from Apocalyptic Texts— Annotated & Explained *Annotation by Robert G. Clouse*
Helps you understand the complex Christian visions of the end of the world.
5½ x 8½, 224 pp, Quality PB, 978-1-59473-170-9 **$16.99**

The Hidden Gospel of Matthew: Annotated & Explained
Translation & Annotation by Ron Miller
Takes you deep into the text cherished around the world to discover the words and events that have the strongest connection to the historical Jesus.
5½ x 8½, 272 pp, Quality PB, 978-1-59473-038-2 **$16.99**

The Lost Sayings of Jesus: Teachings from Ancient Christian, Jewish, Gnostic and Islamic Sources—Annotated & Explained
Translation & Annotation by Andrew Phillip Smith; Foreword by Stephan A. Hoeller
This collection of more than three hundred sayings depicts Jesus as a Wisdom teacher who speaks to people of all faiths as a mystic and spiritual master.
5½ x 8½, 240 pp, Quality PB, 978-1-59473-172-3 **$16.99**

Philokalia: The Eastern Christian Spiritual Texts—Selections Annotated & Explained *Annotation by Allyne Smith; Translation by G. E. H. Palmer, Phillip Sherrard and Bishop Kallistos Ware*
The first approachable introduction to the wisdom of the Philokalia, which is the classic text of Eastern Christian spirituality.
5½ x 8½, 240 pp, Quality PB, 978-1-59473-103-7 **$16.99**

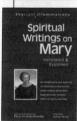

Spiritual Writings on Mary: Annotated & Explained
Annotation by Mary Ford-Grabowsky; Foreword by Andrew Harvey
Examines the role of Mary, the mother of Jesus, as a source of inspiration in history and in life today. 5½ x 8½, 288 pp, Quality PB, 978-1-59473-001-6 **$16.99**

The Way of a Pilgrim: Annotated & Explained
Translation & Annotation by Gleb Pokrovsky; Foreword by Andrew Harvey
This classic of Russian spirituality is the delightful account of one man who sets out to learn the prayer of the heart, also known as the "Jesus prayer."
5½ x 8½, 160 pp, Illus., Quality PB, 978-1-893361-31-7 **$14.95**

MORMONISM

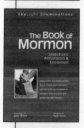

The Book of Mormon: Selections Annotated & Explained
Annotation by Jana Riess; Foreword by Phyllis Tickle
Explores the sacred epic that is cherished by more than twelve million members of the LDS church as the keystone of their faith.
5½ x 8½ , 272 pp, Quality PB, 978-1-59473-076-4 **$16.99**

NATIVE AMERICAN

Native American Stories of the Sacred: Annotated & Explained
Retold & Annotated by Evan T. Pritchard
Intended for more than entertainment, these teaching tales contain elegantly simple illustrations of time-honored truths.
5½ x 8½, 272 pp, Quality PB, 978-1-59473-112-9 **$16.99**

Sacred Texts—cont.

GNOSTICISM

The Gospel of Philip: Annotated & Explained
Translation & Annotation by Andrew Phillip Smith; Foreword by Stevan Davies
Reveals otherwise unrecorded sayings of Jesus and fragments of Gnostic mythology.
5½ x 8½, 160 pp, Quality PB, 978-1-59473-111-2 **$16.99**

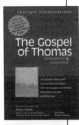

The Gospel of Thomas: Annotated & Explained
Translation & Annotation by Stevan Davies Sheds new light on the origins of Christianity and
portrays Jesus as a wisdom-loving sage. 5½ x 8½, 192 pp, Quality PB, 978-1-893361-45-4 **$16.99**

The Secret Book of John: The Gnostic Gospel—Annotated & Explained
Translation & Annotation by Stevan Davies The most significant and influential text of
the ancient Gnostic religion. 5½ x 8½, 208 pp, Quality PB, 978-1-59473-082-5 **$16.99**

JUDAISM

The Divine Feminine in Biblical Wisdom Literature
Selections Annotated & Explained
Translation & Annotation by Rabbi Rami Shapiro; Foreword by Rev. Cynthia Bourgeault, PhD
Uses the Hebrew books of Psalms, Proverbs, Song of Songs, Ecclesiastes and Job,
Wisdom literature and the Wisdom of Solomon to clarify who Wisdom is.
5½ x 8½, 240 pp, Quality PB, 978-1-59473-109-9 **$16.99**

Ethics of the Sages: *Pirke Avot*—Annotated & Explained
Translation & Annotation by Rabbi Rami Shapiro Clarifies the ethical teachings of the
early Rabbis. 5½ x 8½, 192 pp, Quality PB, 978-1-59473-207-2 **$16.99**

Hasidic Tales: Annotated & Explained
Translation & Annotation by Rabbi Rami Shapiro
Introduces the legendary tales of the impassioned Hasidic rabbis, presenting them as
stories rather than as parables. 5½ x 8½, 240 pp, Quality PB, 978-1-893361-86-7 **$16.95**

The Hebrew Prophets: Selections Annotated & Explained
Translation & Annotation by Rabbi Rami Shapiro; Foreword by Zalman M. Schachter-Shalomi
Focuses on the central themes covered by all the Hebrew prophets.
5½ x 8½, 224 pp, Quality PB, 978-1-59473-037-5 **$16.99**

Zohar: Annotated & Explained *Translation & Annotation by Daniel C. Matt*
The best-selling author of *The Essential Kabbalah* brings together in one place the most
important teachings of the Zohar, the canonical text of Jewish mystical tradition.
5½ x 8½, 176 pp, Quality PB, 978-1-893361-51-5 **$15.99**

EASTERN RELIGIONS

Bhagavad Gita: Annotated & Explained *Translation by Shri Purohit Swami*
Annotation by Kendra Crossen Burroughs Explains references and philosophical terms,
shares the interpretations of famous spiritual leaders and scholars, and more.
5½ x 8½, 192 pp, Quality PB, 978-1-893361-28-7 **$16.95**

Dhammapada: Annotated & Explained *Translation by Max Müller and revised by*
Jack Maguire; Annotation by Jack Maguire Contains all of Buddhism's key teachings.
5½ x 8½, 160 pp, b/w photos, Quality PB, 978-1-893361-42-3 **$14.95**

Rumi and Islam: Selections from His Stories, Poems, and Discourses—
Annotated & Explained *Translation & Annotation by Ibrahim Gamard*
Focuses on Rumi's place within the Sufi tradition of Islam, providing insight into
the mystical side of the religion. 5½ x 8½, 240 pp, Quality PB, 978-1-59473-002-3 **$15.99**

Selections from the Gospel of Sri Ramakrishna: Annotated & Explained
Translation by Swami Nikhilananda; Annotation by Kendra Crossen Burroughs
Introduces the fascinating world of the Indian mystic and the universal appeal
of his message. 5½ x 8½, 240 pp, b/w photos, Quality PB, 978-1-893361-46-1 **$16.95**

Tao Te Ching: Annotated & Explained *Translation & Annotation by Derek Lin*
Foreword by Lama Surya Das Introduces an Eastern classic in an accessible, poetic
and completely original way. 5½ x 8½, 192 pp, Quality PB, 978-1-59473-204-1 **$16.99**

Spirituality

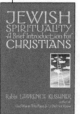

Jewish Spirituality: A Brief Introduction for Christians *by Lawrence Kushner*
5½ x 8½, 112 pp, Quality PB, 978-1-58023-150-5 **$12.95** *(a Jewish Lights book)*

Journeys of Simplicity: Traveling Light with Thomas Merton, Bashō, Edward Abbey, Annie Dillard & Others *by Philip Harnden* 5 x 7¼, 128 pp, HC, 978-1-893361-76-8 **$16.95**

Keeping Spiritual Balance As We Grow Older: More than 65 Creative Ways to Use Purpose, Prayer, and the Power of Spirit to Build a Meaningful Retirement *by Molly and Bernie Srode* 8 x 8, 224 pp, Quality PB, 978-1-59473-042-9 **$16.99**

The Monks of Mount Athos: A Western Monk's Extraordinary Spiritual Journey on Eastern Holy Ground *by M. Basil Pennington, ocso; Foreword by Archimandrite Dionysios*
6 x 9, 256 pp, 10+ b/w line drawings, Quality PB, 978-1-893361-78-2 **$18.95**

One God Clapping: The Spiritual Path of a Zen Rabbi *by Alan Lew with Sherril Jaffe*
5½ x 8½, 336 pp, Quality PB, 978-1-58023-115-2 **$16.95** *(a Jewish Lights book)*

Prayer for People Who Think Too Much: A Guide to Everyday, Anywhere Prayer from the World's Faith Traditions *by Mitch Finley*
5½ x 8½, 224 pp, Quality PB, 978-1-893361-21-8 **$16.99**; HC, 978-1-893361-00-3 **$21.95**

Show Me Your Way: The Complete Guide to Exploring Interfaith Spiritual Direction
by Howard A. Addison 5½ x 8½, 240 pp, Quality PB, 978-1-893361-41-6 **$16.95**

Spirituality 101: The Indispensable Guide to Keeping—or Finding—Your Spiritual Life on Campus *by Harriet L. Schwartz, with contributions from college students at nearly thirty campuses across the United States* 6 x 9, 272 pp, Quality PB, 978-1-59473-000-9 **$16.99**

Spiritually Incorrect: Finding God in All the *Wrong* Places *by Dan Wakefield; Illus. by Marian DelVecchio* 5½ x 8½, 192 pp, b/w illus., Quality PB, 978-1-59473-137-2 **$15.99**

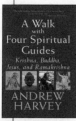

Spiritual Manifestos: Visions for Renewed Religious Life in America from Young Spiritual Leaders of Many Faiths *Edited by Niles Elliot Goldstein; Preface by Martin E. Marty*
6 x 9, 256 pp, HC, 978-1-893361-09-6 **$21.95**

A Walk with Four Spiritual Guides: Krishna, Buddha, Jesus, and Ramakrishna
by Andrew Harvey 5½ x 8½, 192 pp, 10 b/w photos & illus., Quality PB, 978-1-59473-138-9 **$15.99**

What Matters: Spiritual Nourishment for Head and Heart
by Frederick Franck 5 x 7¼, 128 pp, 50+ b/w illus., HC, 978-1-59473-013-9 **$16.99**

Who Is My God?, 2nd Edition: An Innovative Guide to Finding Your Spiritual Identity
Created by the Editors at SkyLight Paths 6 x 9, 160 pp, Quality PB, 978-1-59473-014-6 **$15.99**

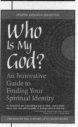

Spirituality—A Week Inside

Come and Sit: A Week Inside Meditation Centers
by Marcia Z. Nelson; Foreword by Wayne Teasdale
The insider's guide to meditation in a variety of different spiritual traditions—Buddhist, Hindu, Christian, Jewish, and Sufi traditions.
6 x 9, 224 pp, b/w photos, Quality PB, 978-1-893361-35-5 **$16.95**

Lighting the Lamp of Wisdom: A Week Inside a Yoga Ashram
by John Ittner; Foreword by Dr. David Frawley
This insider's guide to Hindu spiritual life takes you into a typical week of retreat inside a yoga ashram to demystify the experience and show you what to expect.
6 x 9, 192 pp, 10+ b/w photos, Quality PB, 978-1-893361-52-2 **$15.95**

Making a Heart for God: A Week Inside a Catholic Monastery
by Dianne Aprile; Foreword by Brother Patrick Hart, ocso
Takes you to the Abbey of Gethsemani—the Trappist monastery in Kentucky that was home to author Thomas Merton—to explore the details.
6 x 9, 224 pp, b/w photos, Quality PB, 978-1-893361-49-2 **$16.95**

Waking Up: A Week Inside a Zen Monastery
by Jack Maguire; Foreword by John Daido Loori, Roshi
An essential guide to what it's like to spend a week inside a Zen Buddhist monastery.
6 x 9, 224 pp, b/w photos, Quality PB, 978-1-893361-55-3 **$16.95**
HC, 978-1-893361-13-3 **$21.95**

Meditation / Prayer

Prayers to an Evolutionary God
by William Cleary; Afterword by Diarmuid O'Murchu

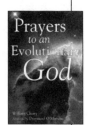

How is it possible to pray when God is dislocated from heaven, dispersed all around us, and more of a creative force than an all-knowing father? Inspired by the spiritual and scientific teachings of Diarmuid O'Murchu and Teilhard de Chardin, Cleary reveals that religion and science can be combined to create an expanding view of the universe—an evolutionary faith.
6 x 9, 208 pp, HC, 978-1-59473-006-1 **$21.99**

Psalms: A Spiritual Commentary
by M. Basil Pennington, ocso; Illustrations by Phillip Ratner

Showing how the Psalms give profound and candid expression to both our highest aspirations and our deepest pain, the late, highly respected Cistercian Abbot M. Basil Pennington shares his reflections on some of the most beloved passages from the Bible's most widely read book.
6 x 9, 176 pp, HC, 24 full-page b/w illus., 978-1-59473-141-9 **$19.99**

The Song of Songs: A Spiritual Commentary
by M. Basil Pennington, OCSO; Illustrations by Phillip Ratner

Join the late M. Basil Pennington as he ruminates on the Bible's most challenging mystical text. Follow a path into the Songs that weaves through his inspired words and the evocative drawings of Jewish artist Phillip Ratner—a path that reveals your own humanity and leads to the deepest delight of your soul.
6 x 9, 160 pp, HC, 14 b/w illus., 978-1-59473-004-7 **$19.99**

Women of Color Pray: Voices of Strength, Faith, Healing,
Hope and Courage *Edited and with Introductions by Christal M. Jackson*
Through these prayers, poetry, lyrics, meditations and affirmations, you will share in the strong and undeniable connection women of color share with God. It will challenge you to explore new ways of prayerful expression.
5 x 7¼, 208 pp, Quality PB, 978-1-59473-077-1 **$15.99**

The Art of Public Prayer: Not for Clergy Only
by Lawrence A. Hoffman
An ecumenical resource for all people looking to change hardened worship patterns.
6 x 9, 288 pp, Quality PB, 978-1-893361-06-5 **$18.99**

Finding Grace at the Center, 3rd Ed.: The Beginning of Centering Prayer
by M. Basil Pennington, ocso, Thomas Keating, ocso, and Thomas E. Clarke, sj
Foreword by Rev. Cynthia Bourgeault, PhD
5 x 7¼, 128 pp, Quality PB, 978-1-59473-182-2 **$12.99**

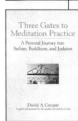

A Heart of Stillness: A Complete Guide to Learning the Art of Meditation
by David A. Cooper 5½ x 8½, 272 pp, Quality PB, 978-1-893361-03-4 **$16.95**

Meditation without Gurus: A Guide to the Heart of Practice
by Clark Strand 5½ x 8½, 192 pp, Quality PB, 978-1-893361-93-5 **$16.95**

Praying with Our Hands: 21 Practices of Embodied Prayer from the World's
Spiritual Traditions *by Jon M. Sweeney; Photographs by Jennifer J. Wilson; Foreword by Mother Tessa Bielecki; Afterword by Taitetsu Unno, PhD*
8 x 8, 96 pp, 22 duotone photos, Quality PB, 978-1-893361-16-4 **$16.95**

Silence, Simplicity & Solitude: A Complete Guide to Spiritual Retreat at Home
by David A. Cooper 5½ x 8½, 336 pp, Quality PB, 978-1-893361-04-1 **$16.95**

Three Gates to Meditation Practice: A Personal Journey into Sufism, Buddhism,
and Judaism *by David A. Cooper* 5½ x 8½, 240 pp, Quality PB, 978-1-893361-22-5 **$16.95**

Women Pray: Voices through the Ages, from Many Faiths, Cultures and Traditions
Edited and with Introductions by Monica Furlong
5 x 7¼, 256 pp, Quality PB, 978-1-59473-071-9 **$15.99**
Deluxe HC with ribbon marker, 978-1-893361-25-6 **$19.95**

Spirituality & Crafts

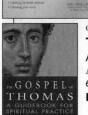

The Knitting Way: A Guide to Spiritual Self-Discovery
by Linda Skolnik and Janice MacDaniels
7 x 9, 240 pp, Quality PB, 978-1-59473-079-5 **$16.99**

The Quilting Path
A Guide to Spiritual Discovery through Fabric, Thread and Kabbalah
by Louise Silk
7 x 9, 192 pp, Quality PB, 978-1-59473-206-5 **$16.99**

Spiritual Practice

Divining the Body
Reclaim the Holiness of Your Physical Self *by Jan Phillips*
A practical and inspiring guidebook for connecting the body and soul in spiritual practice. Leads you into a milieu of reverence, mystery and delight, helping you discover your body as a pathway to the Divine.
8 x 8, 256 pp, Quality PB, 978-1-59473-080-1 **$16.99**

Finding Time for the Timeless: Spirituality in the Workweek
by John McQuiston II
Simple, refreshing stories that provide you with examples of how you can refocus and enrich your daily life using prayer or meditation, ritual and other forms of spiritual practice. 5½ x 6¾, 208 pp, HC, 978-1-59473-035-1 **$17.99**

The Gospel of Thomas
A Guidebook for Spiritual Practice *by Ron Miller; Translations by Stevan Davies*
An innovative guide to bring a new spiritual classic into daily life.
6 x 9, 160 pp, Quality PB, 978-1-59473-047-4 **$14.99**

Earth, Water, Fire, and Air: Essential Ways of Connecting to Spirit
by Cait Johnson 6 x 9, 224 pp, HC, 978-1-893361-65-2 **$19.95**

Labyrinths from the Outside In: Walking to Spiritual Insight—A Beginner's Guide
by Donna Schaper and Carole Ann Camp
6 x 9, 208 pp, b/w illus. and photos, Quality PB, 978-1-893361-18-8 **$16.95**

Practicing the Sacred Art of Listening: A Guide to Enrich Your Relationships and Kindle Your Spiritual Life—The Listening Center Workshop
by Kay Lindahl 8 x 8, 176 pp, Quality PB, 978-1-893361-85-0 **$16.95**

Releasing the Creative Spirit: Unleash the Creativity in Your Life
by Dan Wakefield 7 x 10, 256 pp, Quality PB, 978-1-893361-36-2 **$16.95**

The Sacred Art of Bowing: Preparing to Practice
by Andi Young 5½ x 8½, 128 pp, b/w illus., Quality PB, 978-1-893361-82-9 **$14.95**

The Sacred Art of Chant: Preparing to Practice
by Ana Hernández 5½ x 8½, 192 pp, Quality PB, 978-1-59473-036-8 **$15.99**

The Sacred Art of Fasting: Preparing to Practice
by Thomas Ryan, CSP 5½ x 8½, 192 pp, Quality PB, 978-1-59473-078-8 **$15.99**

The Sacred Art of Forgiveness: Forgiving Ourselves and Others through God's Grace
by Marcia Ford 8 x 8, 176 pp, Quality PB, 978-1-59473-175-4 **$16.99**

The Sacred Art of Listening: Forty Reflections for Cultivating a Spiritual Practice
by Kay Lindahl; Illustrations by Amy Schnapper
8 x 8, 160 pp, b/w illus., Quality PB, 978-1-893361-44-7 **$16.99**

The Sacred Art of Lovingkindness: Preparing to Practice
by Rabbi Rami Shapiro; Foreword by Marcia Ford
5½ x 8½, 176 pp, Quality PB, 978-1-59473-151-8 **$16.99**

Sacred Speech: A Practical Guide for Keeping Spirit in Your Speech
by Rev. Donna Schaper 6 x 9, 176 pp, Quality PB, 978-1-59473-068-9 **$15.99**
HC, 978-1-893361-74-4 **$21.95**

Spirituality of the Seasons

Autumn: A Spiritual Biography of the Season
Edited by Gary Schmidt and Susan M. Felch; Illustrations by Mary Azarian
Rejoice in autumn as a time of preparation and reflection. Includes Wendell Berry, David James Duncan, Robert Frost, A. Bartlett Giamatti, E. B. White, P. D. James, Julian of Norwich, Garret Keizer, Tracy Kidder, Anne Lamott, May Sarton.
6 x 9, 320 pp, 5 b/w illus., Quality PB, 978-1-59473-118-1 **$18.99**
HC, 978-1-59473-005-4 **$22.99**

Spring: A Spiritual Biography of the Season

Edited by Gary Schmidt and Susan M. Felch; Illustrations by Mary Azarian
Explore the gentle unfurling of spring and reflect on how nature celebrates rebirth and renewal. Includes Jane Kenyon, Lucy Larcom, Harry Thurston, Nathaniel Hawthorne, Noel Perrin, Annie Dillard, Martha Ballard, Barbara Kingsolver, Dorothy Wordsworth, Donald Hall, David Brill, Lionel Basney, Isak Dinesen, Paul Laurence Dunbar.
6 x 9, 352 pp, 6 b/w illus., HC, 978-1-59473-114-3 **$21.99**

Summer: A Spiritual Biography of the Season

Edited by Gary Schmidt and Susan M. Felch; Illustrations by Barry Moser
"A sumptuous banquet.... These selections lift up an exquisite wholeness found within an everyday sophistication."— ★ *Publishers Weekly* starred review
Includes Anne Lamott, Luci Shaw, Ray Bradbury, Richard Selzer, Thomas Lynch, Walt Whitman, Carl Sandburg, Sherman Alexie, Madeleine L'Engle, Jamaica Kincaid.
6 x 9, 304 pp, 5 b/w illus., HC, 978-1-59473-083-2 **$21.99**

Winter: A Spiritual Biography of the Season
Edited by Gary Schmidt and Susan M. Felch; Illustrations by Barry Moser
"This outstanding anthology features top-flight nature and spirituality writers on the fierce, inexorable season of winter.... Remarkably lively and warm, despite the icy subject." — ★ *Publishers Weekly* starred review.
Includes Will Campbell, Rachel Carson, Annie Dillard, Donald Hall, Ron Hansen, Jane Kenyon, Jamaica Kincaid, Barry Lopez, Kathleen Norris, John Updike, E. B. White.
6 x 9, 288 pp, 6 b/w illus., Deluxe PB w/flaps, 978-1-893361-92-8 **$18.95**
HC, 978-1-893361-53-9 **$21.95**

Spirituality / Animal Companions

Blessing the Animals: Prayers and Ceremonies to Celebrate God's Creatures, Wild and Tame *Edited by Lynn L Caruso* 5 x 7¼, 256 pp, HC, 978-1-59473-145-7 **$19.99**

What Animals Can Teach Us about Spirituality: Inspiring Lessons from Wild and Tame Creatures *by Diana L. Guerrero* 6 x 9, 176 pp, Quality PB, 978-1-893361-84-3 **$16.95**

Spirituality

Awakening the Spirit, Inspiring the Soul
30 Stories of Interspiritual Discovery in the Community of Faiths
Edited by Brother Wayne Teasdale and Martha Howard, MD; Foreword by Joan Borysenko, PhD
Thirty original spiritual mini-autobiographies showcase the varied ways that people come to faith—and what that means—in today's multi-religious world.
6 x 9, 224 pp, HC, 978-1-59473-039-9 **$21.99**

The Alphabet of Paradise: An A–Z of Spirituality for Everyday Life
by Howard Cooper 5 x 7¼, 224 pp, Quality PB, 978-1-893361-80-5 **$16.95**

Creating a Spiritual Retirement: A Guide to the Unseen Possibilities in Our Lives

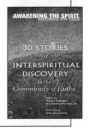

by Molly Srode 6 x 9, 208 pp, b/w photos, Quality PB, 978-1-59473-050-4 **$14.99**
HC, 978-1-893361-75-1 **$19.95**

Finding Hope: Cultivating God's Gift of a Hopeful Spirit
by Marcia Ford 8 x 8, 200 pp, Quality PB, 978-1-59473-211-9 **$16.99**

The Geography of Faith: Underground Conversations on Religious, Political and Social Change *by Daniel Berrigan and Robert Coles* 6 x 9, 224 pp, Quality PB, 978-1-893361-40-9 **$16.95**

God Within: Our Spiritual Future—As Told by Today's New Adults *Edited by Jon M. Sweeney and the Editors at SkyLight Paths* 6 x 9, 176 pp, Quality PB, 978-1-893361-15-7 **$14.95**

About SKYLIGHT PATHS Publishing

SkyLight Paths Publishing is creating a place where people of different spiritual traditions come together for challenge and inspiration, a place where we can help each other understand the mystery that lies at the heart of our existence.

Through spirituality, our religious beliefs are increasingly becoming a part of our lives—rather than *apart* from our lives. While many of us may be more interested than ever in spiritual growth, we may be less firmly planted in traditional religion. Yet, we do want to deepen our relationship to the sacred, to learn from our own as well as from other faith traditions, and to practice in new ways.

SkyLight Paths sees both believers and seekers as a community that increasingly transcends traditional boundaries of religion and denomination—people wanting to learn from each other, *walking together, finding the way.*

For your information and convenience, at the back of this book we have provided a list of other SkyLight Paths books you might find interesting and useful. They cover the following subjects:

Buddhism / Zen	Gnosticism	Mysticism
Catholicism	Hinduism /	Poetry
Children's Books	Vedanta	Prayer
Christianity	Inspiration	Religious Etiquette
Comparative	Islam / Sufism	Retirement
Religion	Judaism / Kabbalah /	Spiritual Biography
Current Events	Enneagram	Spiritual Direction
Earth-Based	Meditation	Spirituality
Spirituality	Midrash Fiction	Women's Interest
Global Spiritual	Monasticism	Worship
Perspectives		

Or phone, fax, mail or e-mail to: SKYLIGHT PATHS Publishing
Sunset Farm Offices, Route 4 • P.O. Box 237 • Woodstock, Vermont 05091
Tel: (802) 457-4000 • Fax: (802) 457-4004 • www.skylightpaths.com
Credit card orders: (800) 962-4544 (8:30AM–5:30PM ET Monday–Friday)
Generous discounts on quantity orders. SATISFACTION GUARANTEED. Prices subject to change.